Totally God's 4 Life

Megan Clinton

HARVEST HOUSE PUBLISHERS

EUGENE, OREGON

Cover by Koechel Peterson & Associates, Inc., Minneapolis, Minnesota

Cover photo © Stockxpert / Jupiterimages Unlimited

All emphasis in Scripture quotations is added by the author.

TOTALLY GOD'S 4 LIFE DEVOTIONAL
Copyright © 2009 by Megan Clinton
Published by Harvest House Publishers
Eugene, Oregon 97402
www.harvesthousepublishers.com

Library of Congress Cataloging-in-Publication Data
    Clinton, Megan
    Totally God's 4 life devotional / Megan Clinton.
        p. cm.
    ISBN 978-0-7369-2760-4 (pbk.)
    1. Teenage girls—Prayers and devotions. 2. Christian teenagers—Prayers and devotions.
I. Title. II. Title: Totally God's for life devotional.
    BV4860.C55 2009
    242'.833—dc22

                                                    2009016112

Printed in the United States of America

        09 10 11 12 13 14 15 16 17 / VP-SK / 10 9 8 7 6 5 4 3 2

Acknowledgments

I am a little pencil in the hand of a writing God
who is sending a love letter to the world.
Mother Teresa

I love this quote. My mom used it in a book, and I wanted to use it too. It reminds me of how small we are compared to the large and majestic God who loves us so much. And how He uses each of us in different roles to carry out His message of love to the world.

A special thank you to Laree Lindburg for your willingness to help me with this devotional. Your time and wisdom are so much appreciated.

Kudos to Harvest House Publishers for your support and dedication. In particular to Terry Glaspey, Carolyn McCready, and Gene Skinner for providing a special platform to reach young women all across America.

To Joshua Straub, Amy Feigel, and Laura Faidley for your editing, writing, research, and insight—you guys are a great help!

And to my parents. I love you both so much and wouldn't be where I am today without your faithful prayers and love for me. I can write a devotional only because of your faithfulness and commitment to raise me with the love of God. You have been living examples of what it means to be totally His!

Contents

Introduction

I've been thinking about you a lot lately—yes, really.

I have tried to imagine what you look like, how you feel about yourself, and where you live. Mostly I have been wondering about what's been on your heart lately. The stuff you think about when no one else is around.

Have you ever wondered at times about God—who He is, whether He really knows you and loves you, how He wants you to respond to difficult life situations, and if He is disappointed in you or simply there for you?

When you listen to people speak about God and life, everyone has an opinion, but real answers seem hard to come by.

As I was thinking about what I should tell you right up front, I was drawn to share some of my favorite Bible verses with you—the ones that have really encouraged me:

- "The name of the LORD is a strong tower; the righteous run to it and are safe" (Proverbs 18:10).

- "Now listen, daughter, don't miss a word: Forget your country, put your home behind you. Be here—the king is wild for you. Since he's your Lord, adore him" (Psalm 45:10-11 MSG).

- "Your word is a lamp to my feet and a light for my path. I have taken an oath and confirmed it, that I will follow your righteous laws. I have suffered much; preserve my life, O LORD, according to your word. Accept, O LORD, the willing praise of my mouth, and teach me your laws. Though I constantly take my life in my hands, I will not forget your law. The wicked have set a snare for me, but I have not strayed from your precepts. Your statutes are my heritage forever; they are the joy of my heart. My heart is set on keeping your decrees to the very end" (Psalm 119:105-112).

- "His wisdom is profound, his power is vast. Who has resisted him and come out unscathed?" (Job 9:4).

- "Why spend money on what is not bread, and your labor on what does not satisfy? Listen, listen to me, and eat what is good, and your soul will delight in the richest of fare" (Isaiah 55:2).

- "'For I know the plans I have for you,' declares the LORD, 'plans to prosper you and not to harm you, plans to give you hope and future'" (Jeremiah 29:11).

As you read, I want you to know that God loves you, and I believe He has a dream for your life. The Bible even says he is wild about you. I really like that. I wrote this devotional because I want you to know that regardless of the situation you find yourself in, God is there in the middle of it all and promises to see you through.

As for me, I am just crazy enough to believe that if you will search and reach for Him, if you will press in close to Him, you will find Him, and He will be your rock, your strong tower.

That's why I want to be totally God's, and I pray you will be too.

Warmly,

1

WHO IS GOD?

Devotions to help us better understand who He is

Who Is God, Really?

*God said to Moses, "I AM WHO I AM. This is what you
are to say to the Israelites: I AM has sent me to you."*
EXODUS 3:14

D id you know that the Bible includes more than 100 names for God?
And that doesn't even count the variations to these names! Whew!
Another bit of trivia—How many words do you think are in the English language?

> 50,000?
> 75,000?
> 100,000?

Try 171, 476! Plus another 47,156 words we don't really use. That's getting close to a quarter of a million words in the English language! But out of all the words in the English language, one will always stand out above all the rest: *God*!

Let's take a look at a few of the many names of our one God:

> *Jehovah*—I Am. One who always exists, eternal and unchangeable.
> *El-Shaddai*—God Almighty
> *Adonai*—Lord, our master and owner
> *Jehovah-jireh*—Jehovah will provide
> *Jehovah-rophe*—Jehovah heals
> *Jehovah-nissi*—Jehovah, my banner
> *Jehovah-M'Kaddesh*—Jehovah, who sanctifies (forgives)
> *Jehovah-shalom*—Jehovah, our peace
> *Jehovah-tsidekenu*—Jehovah, our righteousness
> *Jehovah-rohi*—Jehovah, my Shepherd
> *Jehovah-shammah*—Jehovah is there

By learning the names of God, we get to know a little more about His character. Studying the original usage of God's names is helpful because today the words *God* or *Lord* mean simply "supreme being" or "sovereign of the universe." That's great, but God is so much more!

I don't know about you, but reading the names of God gives me joy! When I am scared, thinking about the names *Jehovah-shalom* and *Jehovah-shammah* makes me feel safe. When I'm worried or nervous, the names *Jehovah-jireh* and *Jehovah-rohi* remind me of God's care.

When my heart is broken or a family member has a terrible illness, the name *Jehovah-rophe* reassures me that regardless of what happens, God will heal in the way He thinks is best. And during crazy, unpredictable times in our world, just the name *Jehovah* fills me with comfort. He has always existed, He is eternal, and He is unchangeable. I love that, especially when something major seems to be shifting in our world every day. God doesn't budge.

His love for us does not change either, and that is very cool. Even when we are unfaithful to Him, He will stay faithful to His word—and to us.

By calling Himself *I Am*, God assures us that He has always been. He is righteousness, peace, our Shepherd, the one who is there. He's the King of kings and Lord of lords. He is our Prince of Peace, our Mighty God and Everlasting Father. His name is above all names—that's our God!

What's a Girl to Do?

Try to use God's names in your everyday life, like when you pray. The names are straight from the Bible, so you can use them to talk to God. When you think of the Lord or talk about Him, remember these descriptions of who He is. They will not only help you in tough times but also help others as well. I challenge you to pray using another one of God's names this week.

Totally Talkin' with God

Father, thank You for giving me Your names. Now that I have read these titles, I feel I know You even better. Help me to understand more and more aspects of Your character, Lord. I love You and trust You. In Jesus' name, amen.

Do You Really Know?

*For God so loved the world that He gave His only begotten Son, that
whoever believes in Him shall not perish, but have eternal life.*

JOHN 3:16 NASB

I want to share with you the reason I wrote this little book. If you take only one thing from the entire book, please let it be the words in this devotion. I hope they will help you make the most important decision you will ever make on this earth.

In this book I talk about what it's like to live a life with Jesus at the center. I know that may sound weird, but let me explain.

The story of humanity starts with Adam and Eve. The cool part is that God specifically gave them permission to roam freely and to eat from any tree they wanted—except for one. So what did they do? They did as any young child would do when Mom says "Don't eat that lollipop until after you eat your lunch!" They snuck an apple from the tree and ate from it anyway. From this point on a barrier was placed between God and humans. This barrier, called sin, keeps us from truly relating to God. In fact, after Adam and Eve ate from the tree, they felt guilty and ashamed, and they just hid from God. Have you ever felt that way, as if you just wanted to hide? We all have. That's because when Adam and Eve disobeyed God, their sin affected all of humanity. You and I sin every day. Romans 3:23 says, "For all have sinned and fall short of the glory of God."

But the good news is this: God loved us so much that He sent is only Son to die for us so that the barrier would be lifted! And if we confess to God that we are sinners, believe in Him, and make Him the center of our lives, we will have life in heaven.

If you haven't made this step yet, I encourage you to right now. The following prayer is the most important prayer you'll ever pray. And it's the first step toward becoming totally God's.

Pray this prayer from your heart to God's heart:

*Father, I know I have sinned, and I'm sorry. I am now ready to turn
away from my sinful past and start a new life in You. Please forgive*

*me of my sins. I invite Jesus to be my Savior. I want Him to be the
center of my life and lead it. Please send Your Holy Spirit to help me
obey You and live for You. I pray all this in Jesus' name. Amen.*

If you prayed that prayer, let me be the first to say congratulations!
The Bible says that right now, because you prayed that prayer, all of the
angels in heaven are rejoicing!

Now it's time to focus on your newfound faith in God!

Your next step, through the power of the Holy Spirit, is to learn more
and walk tight with God. Start praying to Him. This requires nothing
more than you just talking to Him. Begin with the prayer at the end of
this devotion. It is a great start! Read the Bible. Go to church. And find
another Christian woman or a group of girls your age you know who can
begin to mentor you and help you understand what having Jesus at the
center of your life is all about.

I love you and I am praying for you! I trust and hope that you are
encouraged and will grow stronger and deeper in your walk with Jesus.
Let's journey together and live with Jesus at the center of our lives, completely and totally God's!

What's a Girl to Do?

If you decided to believe in Jesus for eternal life—celebrate! Your
sins are forgiven! Maybe you already knew Jesus, and this was just a nice
reminder of your salvation. Or maybe you are not ready. If this is true
for you, pray and ask God to speak to you. Ask Him to give you the faith
you need to be saved. He will listen. After all, this is the most important
decision you'll ever make!

Totally Talkin' with God

*Father, thank You for always being there—for listening and for loving me
first. I pray that You would prepare my heart to fully understand who You are
and what You desire from me as Your follower. I want to know You more! Teach
me, Lord. I am so grateful for the free gift of salvation for all who believe in
Jesus. I love You. In Jesus' name I pray. Amen.*

The Creator

By faith, we see the world called into existence by God's word, what we see created by what we don't see.

HEBREWS 11:3 MSG

When you were a kid, did you ever ask where the sun, moon, or world came from? I know I did—a lot. But seriously, this question is big. As followers of Jesus, we believe that the Bible is 100 percent true. No ifs, ands, or buts. And the very first sentence of the Bible makes an important statement: *God created*.

So what, Megan? Well, not everybody believes that God created the world. Some people believe we came from monkeys. (Well, maybe my brother did, but not me!) But the Bible says that God created everything. Genesis says that He just spoke the words, and...*poof*! Plants, animals, birds, water, me, you... You name it, and it just appeared. Do you find that hard to grasp?

God's pretty big, huh? But God didn't just create way back when. When you and I were smaller than the period at the end of this sentence, God began to put us together intricately. Fingers, toes, a heart that beats, a brain way more complex than the biggest computer out there, eye color, curly hair or straight hair... Down to the last little detail, God put you together.

Does that blow your mind? It does mine! You are unique, and no other girl in the entire world is quite like you. Just look at your fingerprint. No two persons are the same!

The apostle Paul says that when we look around our world, everything God created shouts out about the best Artist ever (Psalm 19:1). God made everything for His glory—and He's good!

Think about it—gorgeous flowers, snow-capped mountains, breathtaking sunsets, and even you! Everything exists to point back to how awesome and good God is.

But here's the deal. A lot of people don't believe in God. They think that Jesus, God's Son, was just a good man, a wonderful teacher, a prophet.

Some people think the Bible is just a silly old book. What do you think? Looking around at the beauty and complexity of creation, it's hard for me to believe that it all just happened by chance.

If we believe that God created us as His girls...well, that's a big deal. It's *huge*! It means that God is our Creator. And if He created us, we belong to Him. My life and your life have just one purpose: to point to Him.

Today, take a minute to stop and think about who God *really* is. Go for a walk outside and look around you at some of the masterpieces He has created, like the mountains, rivers, lakes, grass, trees... God doesn't just work magic tricks. He *creates*.

What's a Girl to Do?

This is a challenging topic. Many Christians today are being drawn away from the truth that God really did create the world. This is as good a time as any to pray and ask God to help you to understand and believe in who He is. You will be tempted to agree with other points of view under pressure, but stand firm; our God is the One and only, and He will be so pleased at your faith in Him.

Totally Talkin' with God

Father, I live in a time when people doubt Your ability to create all things. All around me, people take the praise for things only You have done. Father, forgive them. Forgive me when I do the same thing. I want to truly understand You as the Creator of all. Help me, Lord, to stand firm for Your truth. In Jesus' name, amen.

How Far Will God Go for Me?

Is there anyplace I can go to avoid your Spirit? to be out of your sight?
If I climb to the sky, you're there! If I go underground, you're there.
PSALM 139:7-8 MSG

When I was little, I loved to play hide-and-seek. It was always fun to find a place that was all my own. I usually made Zach, my younger brother, try to find me first. Part of the fun was scaring him to death!

But have you ever done something you *knew* was wrong...and then wanted to run and hide? I have. Way back in the Garden of Eden, Adam and Eve hid from God after they sinned. And ever since then, we have been hiding too.

But do you think we can really hide from God? The Bible says we can't. He's always there—always.

Consider that the Lord has looked at your soul and knows your heart. He watches every move you make. He gets your inner thoughts and evaluates where you're headed in life. Before you say a word, He knows what it'll be. It's amazing how well He knows you. (See Psalm 139:1-4).

God knows us intimately. He knows our secrets, and yet He loves us. He may not always love our behavior, but He loves us.

Let me help you understand how great His love is for you. King David, who was known as the man after God's own heart, was close to God. And yet look at all the sins David committed.

- He stole another man's wife.

- He got her pregnant.

- He told the commander of his army to put Uriah (the woman's husband) in the front line and then fall back so he would be killed.

Wait a minute! David, a man who loved God, was an adulterer *and* a murderer? Yes! He repented of his wrongs, and although God forgave him, David still had to endure some harsh consequences for his sin, just as we all do. But he also knew, without a doubt, God's intimate love for him.

God doesn't give up on us when we mess up. Not a chance! The Bible says that God is changing us from the inside out. And what God starts, He always finishes.

Ask God today to help you be a woman after God's own heart.

What's a Girl to Do?

The only way we will know how much God loves us is to read the Bible. Pray and ask God to show you His love for you and to make that love real in your heart. Trust in Him and go far for Him because of how far He has gone for you.

Totally Talkin' with God

Father, I can be so concerned about whom I identify with in this life. Friends, clubs, colleges, music, clothes...the temptation to fit in is everywhere. But what is truly important is identifying with You. I want to know You more, Lord. I want to understand how far You have gone and will go for me, and I want to grow in how far I will go for You. In Jesus' name, amen.

Not a Deadbeat Dad

A father to the fatherless, a defender of the
widows, is God in his holy dwelling.
PSALM 68:5

A few years ago, I went to the Dominican Republic with my dad to visit a girl we sponsor through World Vision. She was so excited to see us, and I was just as happy to see her!

My eyes were opened like never before. I saw poverty, illness, crime, and so much more. I received a much-needed wake-up call about how many blessings I enjoy: a home, a family, a church, food and clothes...The list could go on and on!

You may have noticed I counted family as a blessing. But I know you may live in a family that has serious struggles. Your parents may be divorced, one parent could be absent, or maybe your mom or dad has died. Perhaps you were adopted or are in foster care. There are a lot of reasons why our parents may not be around—especially our dads.

When I looked into this, I found that America is filled with fatherless kids. The statistics I found were astounding:

- Up to 50 percent of former foster kids or probation youth become homeless within the first 18 months of emancipation.
- Youth in foster care are 44 percent less likely to graduate from high school, and after emancipation, 40 to 50 percent never complete high school.
- Girls in foster care are 60 percent more likely to give birth before age 21.
- Forty percent of American kids will wake up in a home tomorrow where their biological fathers do not live.

Fatherless homes add some alarming stats too! They account for 63 percent of youth suicides, 90 percent of homeless and runway children, 71 percent of high school dropouts, 85 percent of youths in prison, and 59 percent of teen mothers.

Even if you have a father, he may not always be around. He may be deployed in the military, working around the clock, or just plain busy. I know that my dad will not be able to be my "everything." That is a job only God can do. A dad's hugs mean so much to a girl's life, but only God can meet the deepest longings inside her. And He is a Father for all.

Take comfort in His promise. Take refuge in His arms. I pray that regardless of your family situation, God will be the Father you have always wanted and the Father you need. He loves you, and if you know Him as your Lord and Savior, you are a daughter of the King. Ask Him to be your Daddy today!

What's a Girl to Do?

If you are fatherless, have hope—you have a perfect Father! God is your Father for all time. Lean on that truth. We will always have a Father whose arms are open wide!

Totally Talkin' with God

Father, I didn't realize just how true that title is. You are my Father forever. Thank You, Lord. And You are not only my Father but also my Savior and so much more. I love You. Be extra close to those who struggle with the loss of a parent, and comfort them. In Jesus' name, amen.

God Says...

Delight yourself in the LORD and he will
give you the desires of your heart.
PSALM 37:4

I just love this verse, don't you? My desires—hmmm, let's see! A boy-friend who's tall and well-built with brown hair like Zac Efron. A lux-ury car, like a brand-new white convertible Mercedes-Benz. A beautiful home on the beach with a cascading eternity pool in the backyard! Yeah! Okay...maybe that's not what this verse is referring to. (But a girl's gotta dream right?)

The first part of this verse is the real key. "Delight yourself in the LORD." When we truly put the Lord first, His desires become ours. Now let's talk about what that means.

As Christians we often struggle with what following the Lord actually entails. At first thought, I imagine following the Lord means going to a far-off country with no running water, lots of bugs, and nasty things to eat. In no way is that a put-down. It takes a special calling and a unique person to serve God as a missionary. What do you imagine when you think of a life totally surrendered to Jesus?

Anyone can commit her way to the Lord, regardless of her age or what she is doing in life. We often think we need to move to a special place for God to use us in His work. The truth is that all of us can become tools for God right where He has placed us. In school, at work, on the court, in the field, in practice, at the bus stop, at home... God wants to use us every-where to minister to those He loves. And He tells us that He'll bless us for being available. If we trust in Him and do good, and if we delight in Him, He promises to give us the desires of our heart. God asks us to commit our ways to Him. When you do, "He will make your righteousness shine like the dawn, the justice of your cause like the noonday sun" (Psalm 37:3-6).

Isn't that awesome? Does this apply for us today? You bet! It totally does. If God sees that we trust in Him and long to do His will, He will bless us.

Here is one warning: God is *not* a genie in a bottle. If you think, *I'll just do as He says so I can get whatever I want*, guess again. It doesn't work that way. God knows our hearts. He sees us truly delight in Him, trust Him, and do good things for Him. We can't trick God into blessing us.

Let's pray and ask God to give us a heart that longs to serve Him as He desires. Let's take our selfish desires out of the equation. Throw our wants aside. When we have done so, God will open our eyes and show us His goodness and His ways. And that will be all the blessing we will ever need!

What's a Girl to Do?

I know this is a tall order, but let's not get discouraged and down about all that God asks of us. Just take it one step at a time. The first thing may be to pray or to deny some of our wants. Maybe you need to work on trusting in Him. He really does want to give you the desires of your heart!

Totally Talkin' with God

Father, I want to know You more. Please plant within my heart the seed to do Your will, trust in You, do good, and delight in You. I know that when I am fully living for you, the desires I have will already be filled—with You! I believe that having Your joy in my life is a huge blessing. I love You! In Jesus' name, amen.

Distractions

Behold, the LORD was passing by! And a great and strong wind
was rending the mountains and breaking in pieces the rocks before
the LORD; but the LORD was not in the wind. And after the wind
an earthquake, but the LORD was not in the earthquake. After
the earthquake a fire, but the LORD was not in the fire; and
after the fire a sound of a gentle blowing...And behold, a voice
came to him and said, "What are you doing here, Elijah?"

1 KINGS 19:11-13 NASB

New York City! One of my most favorite places to visit. Saks, Macy's, H&M, Nordstrom, Banana Republic...all in one location (even if I can't afford to buy anything)!

The only bummer is the constant sounds of city life all around. Police sirens, car horns, construction machinery, truck engines...after a while, I need to get away to a nearby park and separate myself from all the fury. There, I can hear the wind in the trees rustling the leaves and birds chirping in the warm air. Ahh...peace.

I agree with 1 Kings 19. We can sense God's presence in the gentle whisper of a breeze, the soft snore of a newborn baby, the cheep-cheep of fluffy yellow chicks, and the swooshing of sand beneath our feet on the beach. In the quiet moments of our hearts we hear God best.

God is everywhere. The theological term for this is *omnipresent*. Always around. Even when the police sirens pass by, machines pound on concrete, or annoyed people blast their car horns, God is there.

But quiet is hard to come by in this day and age. We'd have to turn off our cell phones, iPods, televisions, and computers. We'd have to leave the city, get away from all the cars, and turn from tons of people. But then again, maybe we just need to go on a walk in the park with our dog or go to our room and shut the door.

Whatever we do, being quiet and listening to God is a choice. There is just something special about being alone and listening for God. It's intimate. He knows it, and we feel it.

Choosing to distance yourself from distractions like phones, computers, and the TV can be difficult and could make you look...well, funny to your friends. But the benefits of alone time with God are incredible. Knowing that the Creator of the universe wants to spend time with you, talk with you, and hear your thoughts and concerns—is anything better than that?

He knows your heart. He knows your future. He knows your fears. He knows your failures—and He loves you anyway. God already knew what Elijah was doing on that mountain, but still He asked. That's how God works! He wants a relationship. Communication. He wants to hear what we have to say even though He already knows our thoughts. He wants you to see Him in the gentle blowing of the wind. He wants to be the sole owner of your heart.

But the choice is yours. Choose to listen. Find a quiet place and meet with Him. Be still and embrace His presence.

What's a Girl to Do?

Getting away from all the distractions in life is hard. We may be able to escape outward things, but shutting off our minds is another task. I find that prayer helps. If I pray or read the Bible, my mind wanders to the things of God and not the world. Try getting away to a quiet place sometime this week and read, pray, and listen. It works for me.

Totally Talkin' with God

Father, You do love me and have called me to be totally Yours. I want to be all Yours, Lord, but I struggle to know what that looks like or how to do it exactly. Teach me Your ways. Open my mind to You during the quiet times so I can know Your voice even in the loud times. I love You, God. In Jesus' name, amen.

God: The Parent

*My son, do not make light of the Lord's discipline, and do not
lose heart when he rebukes you, because the Lord disciplines
those he loves, and he punishes everyone he accepts as a son.*
HEBREWS 12:5-6

My dad and I are close. We share a special father-daughter relationship. When I needed discipline, Dad administered it—not to make my life miserable, but because he loved me. He didn't do it because he was angry at me. This is why I respect him and why we have such a good bond today. Learning from the way he disciplined me has taught me how I want to discipline my own kids someday.

Parents have a tough job. When God gives them a child, they soon realize the extent of the responsibility. This babe can't do anything for himself. Days and nights are spent on the baby's care. But a baby's mistakes are innocent. An infant can't discern danger from safety or right from wrong.

You and I have pretty much outgrown the days of time-outs. But regardless of what age we are, we still experience consequences for our choices. Your mom or dad may not be the one you end up giving account to. It could be a teacher, police officer, or judge.

If you often disobey authority and rebel against control, think about this: Are you rebelling against God as well? I totally understand that you may not have parents who have disciplined you lovingly. You may have even been abused or neglected. And for that, I am terribly sorry. God does not discipline with anger when we mess up or totally defy Him in some way. Rather, He does it because He wants what is best for us. His will is good and acceptable and perfect (Romans 12:2 NASB).

Hebrews 12 encourages us to not brush aside the Lord's discipline. We are to stay positive and not lose heart, because God loves us. He punishes everyone He accepts as sons and daughters (see Hebrews 12:6). In our day, when kids can sue their parents or "divorce" their family, this Bible passage may be difficult to accept. But God's Word is truth.

Whether we have had good parents or bad, God truly loves us, and His discipline is for our own good. He loves us enough to correct our behavior so we will lead lives that please Him.

What's a Girl to Do?

Maybe this devotion has caught you rebelling against those who discipline you. Maybe you have had horrible experiences with discipline. Those don't represent who God is. Open your heart today to the truth: God is love (1 John 4:8).

Totally Talkin' with God

Father, You love me with an everlasting love. I understand that Your discipline is for my good because I am Your child. The way the world sees discipline is so different from the way Your Word describes it. I want to obey You and not rebel. Guide me closer to Your will so that when Your discipline comes, I will accept it and appreciate the love that motivates it. In Jesus' name, amen.

2

THE REAL ME

Devotions to encourage us to be real in Christ

Who Am I?

*Your very lives are a letter that anyone can read just by looking at
you. Christ himself wrote it—not with ink, but with God's living
Spirit; not chiseled into stone, but carved into human lives.*

2 CORINTHIANS 3:2-3 MSG

Texting, Twitter, Facebook—in today's world, connecting is super easy.
I love talking to my friends, staying in touch with my family, and just
looking at pictures of everybody. But sometimes, I can get lost in the
craziness and forget who I am.

Who am I apart from my friends, my schoolwork, my family, and my
youth group? Who is the real me? The real you?

The media tell us some pretty crazy things about how we should think,
feel, and act. I love clothes as much as the next person, but too often we're
led to believe that unless we sport the latest from Hollister and American
Eagle or look just like the girls in *Seventeen* and *Teen Vogue*, we're slacking
in the looks department.

But stop and think about it. Who defines you? Fashions change, and
models get old. But fortunately, God's Word doesn't. My mom always told
me, "You may be the only Bible some of your friends will ever read." The
apostle Paul even wrote that we are human letters from God that communicate His glory to the world around us. This means that God often
uses you and me to get His message of love to other people. I love that!
But it makes me wonder, *Am I living in a way that lets God communicate to
others through my life?*

Who are we? We are God's text messages to the world: "I love you,"
"I've saved you," "You matter to God," "Don't give up hope," "I am here."

Here are some word pictures the Bible uses to describe who we are:

- a chosen people—God's daughters
- a royal priesthood—princesses in God's royal court
- God's own possession—His own treasure (1 Peter 2:9)

- shining stars—set apart in the darkness of this world (Philippians 2:15)
- a sweet aroma of the knowledge of Christ—God's perfume (2 Corinthians 2:14)

That's a pretty amazing list, and it's easy for me to look at it and think, *I'm never gonna measure up to that. I'm just an ordinary girl!* Maybe you're thinking the same thing. But God doesn't wait for us to get our act together before He speaks these words over us.

Right now, regardless of what you've done, if you have trusted in Jesus as your Savior, you are His daughter. You are His princess. You are His treasure. You are His perfume. God's Word says so!

And here's the best part: None of it depends on us. God declares these things about us. The labels we receive from the world every day are usually bogus and hurtful, but the titles God has given us show us who we really are. Our identity depends on our hearts, not our hairdos.

Take some time today to dig into the rich treasure chest of the Bible and discover something new about who you really are—a girl who is totally God's.

Being popular can't even compare.

What's a Girl to Do?

When times get tough, remember all the wonderful names God has for you. You really are special to Him. Let's embrace these truth-filled titles and live out our identity in Christ for all people to know and read.

Totally Talkin' with God

Father, open my eyes so I may see the truth of who I am in You. Satan wants me to forget how beautiful and lovely I am in You. Lord, help me to be strong and boldly display the letter of Christ, which is written on my heart. In Jesus' name, amen.

Labels

Food for the stomach and the stomach for food.
1 CORINTHIANS 6:13

Chubby, unattractive, unathletic—do any of these labels sound familiar? Our obsession with being fit or thin didn't start yesterday. Maybe you were called hurtful names as a child, or maybe your parents pushed you to be skinny.

Or maybe your older sister, who is a size two, got all the attention. Perhaps you're trying to get the attention of your perfect guy. You might even be trying to control your diet in unhealthy ways in an otherwise out-of-control world.

Every day, I see girls who struggle with their weight. Hey, it's a battle for me too! No girl on this planet, regardless of how godly she is, is immune from the insecurity that comes with trying to be picture-perfect. I struggled to keep the infamous "freshman 15" off this year.

It's rough being a girl who is growing into a woman. A million and one different things are going on in our bodies. And a lot of times, we're way too hard on ourselves. But be honest—no two bodies are alike. Each of us was uniquely put together by God (Psalm 139:13). And yet we swear there must be a perfect figure.

"All I want is to be size..."

"I'll be happy if I weigh..."

"Everyone will like me when I look like..."

We talk like this all the time. And somehow, we tend to think that hitting a certain weight or jeans size will make us happy. But it's all lies.

Can we honestly say with the psalmist, "I praise you, for I am fearfully and wonderfully made" (Psalm 139:14 ESV)? Do we really believe that about our bodies?

One of my friends who struggles with bulimia told me, "I can't stop. I don't know what to do...I eat, but all I can think about is getting the food out of me so I won't get fat."

An actress named Tracy Gold had an eating disorder too. Here's how she describes it:

It's a statement of not loving yourself. Your whole world is consumed with how people perceive you and what they're thinking about you. But you can never change what people are going to say about you and think about you. You have to know how you feel about yourself inside.

If you want to beat the labels, you've got to know the truth about yourself—about who God says you are. Spend time memorizing Psalm 139. Allow these truths to sink into your being. Then every time a negative thought about the way you look comes into your mind, you can beat it with the truth!

The Bible says that Jesus is crazy about you. He's so happy, He bursts out in song! (See Zephaniah 3:17.) To be totally God's means giving Jesus complete control of your life—even your diet.

Do you need to peel off some labels today that are actually lies? God's label for you is the best of all: "This is My girl, and I love her." And the best part? It's true.

What's a Girl to Do?

Ask yourself, *Do I believe I am worth fighting for?* That is the real question. Girls die from trying to control their eating. Satan uses this as a tactic to control us. It's all a game—let's sit this one out.

Totally Talkin' with God

Father, I have not loved myself as You tell me to. You are faithful and worthy of praise. You have made me in Your image. Forgive me, Lord. Help me to beat my obsession with looks and weight. In Jesus' name, amen.

Identity Theft

Set your mind on the things above, not on the things that are on earth.
COLOSSIANS 3:2 NASB

A lot of nights alone in bed, I think about being loved, cherished, held. I want somebody to share my life with, to know me—the real me. You too?

My dad often tells me how much he loves me and God loves me. To be honest, I have often struggled with the God part—that He really loves me. I mean, come on. I constantly fall short of who God wants me to be and what He wants me to do. And then I wonder, *How could He love me?*

I believe most girls I know feel the same way and have trouble believing that God really loves them. They may say God loves them, but they do unhealthy things in order to feel loved. Let me explain.

I see girls pursue guys at any cost. They turn their backs on their girlfriends, give up activities they once enjoyed, listen over and over to sappy love songs on their iPods, and daydream about their princes. Many young women are filling themselves with anything to feel loved, ultimately losing their sense of self and their identity. But I want you to know this: Our identity in Christ is secure.

Let me show you what Jesus did. He starts a conversation with Peter that goes something like this: "Look, you are going to deny Me three times before the rooster crows."

Peter says something like, "No way. Even if I have to die with You, I will not deny You" (see Matthew 26:34-35).

Be careful what you say, because pride can often make us put our foot in our mouths. And Peter did just that. After Jesus was taken into the custody of the Jewish leaders to be prosecuted and crucified, Peter did deny Jesus—three times. Afterward, he felt so horrible that he wept bitterly. I'll bet Peter thought he'd lost his identity in Christ.

Here is the amazing part. After Jesus rose from the grave, Mary Magdalene and Mary the mother of James visited Jesus' burial site to anoint Him with spices. When they entered the tomb, a young man wearing a white robe told them that Jesus had risen from the dead. But the point here is this: When he told them the good news that Jesus had risen, he specifically said, "Go tell Jesus' disciples *and Peter*" (Mark 16:5-7).

Did you see what Jesus did? He instructed the angel to personally send a shout-out to Peter so Peter would know that Jesus forgave him.

When I struggle to know that God loves me, I remind myself of Peter. And then I start looking for the "little hugs" God places in my life.

He does the same for you, often through other people: messengers who show you how much God loves you, the encouraging words of a friend, a kind gesture by a stranger, a sweet text message from your mom. Your identity is secure in His love for you. Look for it today.

What's a Girl to Do?

Make an effort this week to consciously focus on God's Word and reminders of His love for you. Look up verses and choose to let Him show you your true identity. When you do, the world's temptations will seem to fade.

Totally Talkin' with God

Father, thank You for loving me and helping me know who I am in You. I fall so easily and tend to focus my eyes on things that bring me down. Help me to fix my eyes on You so my identity is secure in You. In Jesus' name, amen.

Rescued

By grace you have been saved through faith; and that not of yourselves,
it is the gift of God; not as a result of works, so that no one may boast.
EPHESIANS 2:8-9 NASB

As a little girl, I loved to dream of a handsome prince coming to my rescue. In my play world, Ken always fought off the bad guys to keep Barbie safe. I watched *Sleeping Beauty* and *Cinderella* a lot, oftentimes with the secret hope that I too would one day meet my own perfect prince.

But despite Disney's dreamy depictions, I have found that life isn't so predictable and rosy. Even Cinderella and Princess Aurora (who have super big chests and tiny waists...gotta love those animators) have problems. Both princesses seem to be destined for something great, but both are in danger from would-be destroyers.

So Cinderella has no dress to wear to the ball, and Princess Aurora falls under the spell of Carabosse, the wicked fairy godmother.

Each fairy tale has twists and turns, but at the end of the day, only one thing matters: The prince comes. And he and his princess gallop off into the sunset to live happily ever after.

You might be thinking, *But I'm in real life. And real life is so not like fairy tales.*

Or is it? Let me be honest: The evil one wants to keep you and me in prison. But the Prince has come to rescue us so that we may have life (John 10:10).

The apostle Paul says, "He has rescued us from the dominion of darkness and brought us into the kingdom of the Son he loves, in whom we have redemption, the forgiveness of sins" (Colossians 1:13-14).

Jesus has rescued us—not just from a dark castle, but from death and bondage to sin. Sometimes, though, I forget! I forget that I have a real enemy, Satan, who wants to put me in a prison of sin. I forget that I have a real rescuer, Jesus, who has already made a way for me to be saved.

Do you forget sometimes too? Have you forgotten that you're worth saving? Do you feel down and out, as if you're not good enough? As if nobody loves you?

Remember your Rescuer. He took off His royal robes and came down to our level. He took all of God's punishment for our mistakes because we were that important to Him.

Need proof of your worth? Look at the blood of Jesus. I can't even begin to comprehend what Jesus went through on the cross, but I do know one thing. In God's mind, you were worth dying for.

You *are* important—important enough to be loved and rescued from the sick nastiness of the sin that would have destroyed you. Important enough to be totally God's—and totally free! All you have to do is follow Him.

What's a Girl to Do?

If this devotion found you wondering what salvation is, turn back to the very first devotion in this book. Then ask yourself, *Is there any reason why I don't believe this?* If the answer is yes, find some mature believers and keep asking questions as you search for the truth. If the answer is no, trust in Jesus and be rescued from the dominion of darkness.

Totally Talkin' with God

Father, I am amazed by Your love for me. Thank You for this gift of salvation, which comes to me so freely. I don't have to work for it; I just need faith, and faith comes from You. Father, lead me now into a closer walk with You. I long to know You more. In Jesus' name, amen.

True Beauty

What matters is not your outer appearance—the
styling of your hair, the jewelry you wear, the cut of your
clothes—but your inner disposition. Cultivate inner
beauty, the gentle, gracious kind that God delights in.

1 PETER 3:3-4 MSG

Cute purses, snazzy earrings, trendy shoes—I love fun, pretty stuff. Maybe you do too. But I'm learning that those things are just accessories to a deeper feminine beauty that God has already placed in my heart.

Stasi Eldredge shares the meaning of being a girl in her book *Captivating*: "God has set within you a femininity that is powerful and tender, fierce and alluring." I love that! In a culture that tells us to make it big—to be popular, famous, thin—and to get guys' attention, it's easy to get so caught up in this real-life beauty pageant that we forget the beauty we already possess. We don't consider the beauty that really matters to God.

God created you uniquely as a girl. And He created you to be beautiful. After all, everything God created, He called good. But evidently you are more than just good—God is absolutely crazy about you!

How do I know? Because He paid for your sins. He effectively said, "This is how much I love you. This is how beautiful you are. This is how valuable you are to Me." He then stretched out His arms on the cross and died for you! For your mistakes, baggage, and mishaps. For the white lies, big lies, and everything in-between. Even for the stuff nobody knows about.

What does this mean about how we live? I love what Stasi says about a girl who is totally God's: "The gift of our presence is a rare and beautiful gift. To come unguarded, undistracted—and be fully present, fully engaged with whoever we are with at that moment." Jesus, our example, valued the people He talked to. He *really* cared about them. He *really* listened.

And that's what we're called to do too. When we are totally God's, we give the gift of our undivided attention to the people we meet. Not just the stylish girls, the cute guys, or the people we need, but every person. Even those we don't need, and even if they dress differently than we do or talk weird. Christ died for each one.

How often do we judge people based on our first impression? In today's focus verses, Peter says that hairstyles, jewelry, and fashion aren't what really count. Sure, we all love a cute outfit. But Jesus wants us to spend time cultivating inner beauty—the kind that shows up in the way we treat other people. The way we love. The way we act unselfishly. The way we care.

Peter is *not* saying we should walk around with ratty hair and dingy, smelly clothes. A girl who is totally God's takes care of her body because she is a princess of Jesus Christ. But our beauty doesn't depend on how we look. We can be dressed to a *T* but forget the most important part—our hearts.

A girl who is totally God's has a gentle and quiet spirit—a heart that revels in God's love, a heart that loves God first, and a heart that is bubbling over with God's love for every single person.

The next time you pick out an outfit, think about your attitude too. A cute outfit and an ugly, selfish heart just don't match.

What's a Girl to Do?

A gentle and quiet spirit is precious in the sight of God. With that knowledge, pray and ask the Lord to help you become a young woman who desires inner beauty.

Totally Talkin' with God

Father, teach me through Your Word what a gentle and quiet spirit looks like in my life. Renew my mind and transform me so I can realize how precious I am in Your eyes. In Jesus' name, amen.

Whose Body Is It?

Don't you know that you yourselves are God's
temple and that God's Spirit lives in you?
1 CORINTHIANS 3:16

It's my body and I'll do what I want!" The magazine ad I recently read stated exactly what girls believe about their bodies these days. They might say it this way: "It's mine; I can treat it as I want to." Turn on the television, look at a magazine, glance at the Internet, or talk to a friend, and you'll soon come across topics like alcohol and drugs, binging and purging, wearing revealing clothes, and even pornography and casual sex with many partners and both genders.

These all destroy our bodies, which God calls His temple. *Temple?* Yep. It means the place where God lives. In the Old Testament, God's Spirit dwelled in the tabernacle in the wilderness and then the temple in Jerusalem. But when we accept Jesus as our Savior, His Spirit literally moves in—not just for a temporary lease, but forever. God's not renting. He owns you.

What does that mean? That means that you don't own yourself anymore! It's not about knowing *who* you are; it's about knowing *whose* you are. When God sees you, He sees Jesus living in you! That should change the way you see yourself. Paul's message is simple: You belong to God. Period.

You might be thinking, *So what does that mean? I mean, I'm not going to go around wearing a robe and sandals and be a monk.* And I totally agree with you. (I like my heels too much!) But God is telling us we need to look at our bodies differently now that we belong to Him.

You may struggle with some sort of "temple destruction." Maybe you wrestle with an eating disorder or have had sex or are cutting. Or maybe you can't stop getting high or living off of junky foods. Whatever it is, if you are a believer in Jesus Christ, He will help you change the way you live so you can build a healthy, vibrant temple.

You can start by seeking Him, repenting of your ways, and changing your habits. Here's what the Bible says:

> Trust GOD from the bottom of your heart;
> don't try to figure out everything on your own.
> Listen for GOD's voice in everything you do, everywhere you go;
> he's the one who will keep you on track.
> Don't assume that you know it all.
> Run to GOD! Run from evil!
> Your body will glow with health,
> your very bones will vibrate with life! (Proverbs 3:5-8 MSG).

Building healthy temples will make our bodies glow and our bones vibrate with life! And it will change the way we live. Before we run off and do something we might later regret, we need to pray and ask God if what we're about to do (or not do) is healthy for us. That might mean saying no to what your friends are doing. It may mean getting more sleep or waking up earlier to go exercise.

Whatever the case, make a list of things you need to change to take care of God's temple—your body. Take steps today toward new habits and a vibrant, healthy life in the days ahead.

What's a Girl to Do?

I will repeat the challenge I made above. Ask God His opinion when you are not absolutely sure if you should do something. Even when you think you know the answer, ask Him anyway. Then do what He says. He will be so pleased you consulted Him and then followed through.

Totally Talkin' with God

Father, this world sends me confusing signals about what is right and wrong. Help me to rely on Your guidance for daily decisions that may have spiritual consequences. I am excited to grow in this area of my relationship with You. In Jesus' name, amen.

Where Is Your Heart?

For where your treasure is, there your heart will be also.
MATTHEW 6:21

When I think of treasure, I think of pirates: buried chests of gold, deserted islands, and Johnny Depp as Captain Jack Sparrow.

But in today's verse, Jesus is talking about something much more valuable than gold. He's talking about how to take care of our hearts.

I *love* going to the mall. Just ask my mom or my best friend! But in this passage, Jesus challenges us to not waste our time storing up or placing too much value on things here on earth. Remember that cute shirt you *had* to have last spring? Do you still have it? Maybe you do, or maybe you don't. It may be a little bit threadbare or even stained. Stuff is just stuff, and it will probably get lost, worn out, or thrown away. It might even somehow disappear into a roommate's closet!

Depressing? No, because Jesus wants us to focus on packing treasure for heaven. God knows how we girls are. The way that we spend our money and our time reveals and even helps determine the desires of our hearts (Matthew 6:19-21). My mom always told me, "If you want to figure out who a girl really is, look at the way she spends her money!"

It's true. Money is a big deal. In fact, Jesus said, "You cannot serve both God and money" (Matthew 6:24). Ouch.

Jesus encouraged His followers (including us girls) to sell their possessions and give to the poor. That doesn't mean Jesus was saying we should never have any money or nice possessions. Rather, He was driving at the *love* of "stuff." It can wield unbelievable power in our minds. And it's easy for a girl to think that money, clothes, or boyfriends will keep us happy. But they won't.

So what's a girl to do?

We need to stop focusing on ourselves. I have come to believe that we build treasures in heaven by giving, not by getting. Taking the time to care about other people—the hurting people in our lives—is the "gold" we can store in heaven. It yields the treasure that lasts forever.

Why is it so hard to live this way? One word: *Satan*.

We are in a battle against evil spirits, not flesh and blood (Ephesians 6:12). And do you know what Satan wants from us more than anything? The evil one wants us to take our eyes off God. He wants us to break ties with the lover of our souls. How does he most often do it?

You got it—through "stuff."

Are the possessions and money in your life distracting your heart? If you really want to know, look at what's most valuable to you. Is it money or clothes? Cell phones or iPods or other people?

Start packing your bags for heaven. Choose to give, not just to get. That's where today's blessings and eternal treasure lie. And no pirate can touch that—not even Captain Jack Sparrow.

What's a Girl to Do?

Putting Jesus and His will first in our lives can be a real challenge. But I pray we are beginning to understand just how important it is not to become captive to the lies of this world. Let's ask God to reveal areas where we have stored treasures here on earth and not in heaven and see if we can change that.

Totally Talkin' with God

Father, I don't want to be caught as a captive in Satan's lies. Help me to use all I have been given—including my money, skills, and possessions—to do as You tell me. I pray that anything I do will glorify You, Lord, and not myself. All glory to You, God, my Father, my King. In Jesus' name, amen.

Living Free

If God is for us, who can be against us?...In all these things
we are more than conquerors through him who loved us.
ROMANS 8:31,37

I heard the song "Nobody Knows It but Me" the other day, and the words have stuck with me. They describe someone who says he's dying inside, but nobody else knows. Sometimes I feel that way—I can wind up feeling pathetic and ashamed, convinced I'm a loser. And nobody knows it but me. Is that how you would describe yourself? Every girl struggles with something. And a lot of times, we don't talk to anybody about it—not even our best friends.

Is that you? Do you walk around hurting every day, but nobody has a clue? You can hide behind the makeup and clothes, but God knows what's in your heart. And He hurts for you. I believe God weeps over the way our sin or other people's sin twists the lives of His beloved girls.

Maybe your struggle is one we've already talked about. Or maybe it's so taboo that no one ever talks about it, like pornography, cutting, huffing, or even suicidal thoughts. Maybe you were abused by someone you should have been able to trust. Maybe you've been raped, and you haven't told a soul.

As your sister in Christ, I want you to know one thing: God wants you to be free. *But Megan,* you might be thinking, *there's no hope for me. My life is too screwed up.*

God is bigger than your pain. Consider a girl who was sexually abused by her own dad. She grew up hating him for it. Even worse, she hated herself for letting him do it.

For Lori, life was miserable. The only ways she could make herself feel better were to act out sexually or to get high. And so she did, every day. Most girls who grew up in a situation like this will do anything to feel better. According to the stats, Lori *should* have grown up to be promiscuous and to hate men.

Thankfully, God loves broken people. Jesus said, "It is not the healthy who need a doctor, but the sick" (Mark 2:17). This world is far from perfect. And for those who have been sexually abused, or whose parents have divorced, or who have been bullied at school, or who have lost a close friend, life can be particularly dark.

But Jesus came to heal broken hearts. To free people (like you and me) from the chains of sin and injustice (Isaiah 61:1). To proclaim, in effect, "My daughter, you are free." Regardless of what you have done or what has been done to you, you don't have to live in guilt and shame. Jesus took your guilt and shame all the way to the grave and buried it there.

The beautiful truth about God is that when we are most broken, He is closest (Psalm 38:17-22). And He's the only one who can make sense of the mess of our lives.

His love is bigger than any hurt. Jesus didn't just put a Band-Aid on our broken heart...He gives us a new heart. He gives us hope. Learn to let His love in. You don't need all that other stuff to feel okay. This is how we become totally God's.

How about you? What's your story? Satan keeps us in bondage to the hurt in our past by keeping us quiet. Do you want to be free? Find someone you trust, someone you look up to, like your mom, a teacher, or a Christian counselor. Tell that person what's going on. Break the silence and be free.

What's a Girl to Do?

If you are hurting because of abuse, addictions, or loss, don't try to make it alone. Get help now. This is not something to take lightly. I love you, and God does even more than me. Take care of yourself.

Totally Talkin' with God

Father, I know I need help. I know others who need help too. Guide me in wisdom to defeat the enemy at his best work—making me believe I am worthless. I am made in Your image, and You love me. May those truths stick like glue to my heart. In Jesus' name, amen.

3

TOTALLY HIS

Devotions to ground us in our walk with Christ

Faith like a Child's

Now faith is being sure of what we hope for
and certain of what we do not see.

This verse reminds me of when I was five years old and wanted to go off the diving board *so* bad. But it scared me. The water was so deep, I couldn't touch the bottom. My dad would swim to the end of the diving board, hold his hands up high, and say, "Come on, Megan. You can do it! Trust me." I'd hesitate only a few seconds, and then I'd close my eyes, jump, and scream in joy! Splashing into the water, I'd get wet, but I wouldn't drown because my dad was there to catch me. I had faith in my dad. I had hope that he would catch me. I could see him waiting for me.

But what if your dad isn't around? Or what happens when my dad can't be there for me and I have a difficult decision to make? What do I do when I am figuratively standing on the diving board, wondering if I'll sink or swim, and can't see anybody there to catch me?

Most of us tend to make decisions based on our own strength. It's like having floaties on our arms. Our decisions are guided by what we know we can accomplish and where we know we'll stay safe. And we put our faith in those things: our intelligence, good looks, athletic ability, musical talent, a likable personality, or...

But faith in God is more than that. It's standing on the end of the diving board without floaties and without anyone there to catch you, yet you know that when you jump, you'll be okay.

The Bible invites us to have faith like a child (Matthew 18:2-4). Run to the diving board with no holds barred. Step out in faith to make a decision, knowing God has your back, that He is good, and that He will always be looking out for your best interest even when you are hurting.

To be totally God's, we must have faith. Without it, we can't possibly please God, because anyone who comes to Him must believe that He exists and that He rewards those who seek Him (Hebrews 11:3,6). God is the only one who can fill the hole in our soul, comfort our loneliness, soothe our hurt and pain, forgive us for our mistakes, and guide our decisions.

Consider today what you are placing your faith in more than God. Is anything holding you back from running into His arms and trusting Him with reckless abandon, just as a child would? Write those things on a piece of paper and begin praying over them today, asking God to strengthen your faith in areas where you lack it. He will be pleased that you are faithful enough already to ask Him to strengthen your faith.

What's a Girl to Do?

Faith is a term we have grown up with in the church, but I believe we have forgotten its true importance. A solid relationship with Christ is based on faith alone. Begin to trust in Jesus today.

Totally Talkin' with God

Father, I love You! With all my being I want this to be true. I don't want to live as if I don't believe, because I do. Help my unbelief, Lord. Grow my faith in You! In Jesus' name, amen.

It's a Small World After All

The LORD knows the thoughts of man, that they are a mere breath.
PSALM 94:11 NASB

Do you believe God can heal someone? That He can really reach down and touch a grandparent who has cancer, an aunt who was critically injured in a car accident, or a friend who's hurting so bad, she's cutting?

Or think about this. Do you believe God is there for us in the middle of a family crisis, the loss of a loved one, or a breakup? Is He there when a tornado rips through your neighborhood, tearing apart homes and businesses for miles around?

In the Bible, Job had to face some of these difficult questions about God.

Job desired to please God, to listen to Him and obey Him. The Bible says Job turned away from sin (Job 1:8). Completely blameless and always pure, Job was a man of integrity. But Satan didn't think Job's commitment to God was real. He thought Job was fake. So he challenged God to allow him to test Job and make Job's life straight-up miserable. God agreed to the test, so Satan destroyed Job's life. Here's what he took away from him:

- Job's animals were stolen. A lot of them—7000 sheep, 3000 camels, 500 yoke of oxen, and 500 donkeys. These weren't just animals; they were Job's income.

- All of his workers were killed.

- His seven sons and three daughters were crushed when their house collapsed.

- Job himself got really sick. Big, nasty sores covered his whole body.

And that was in just one day!

But even though Job's life fell apart, he didn't. His wife did though. She told him to curse God and die (Job 2:9). (Marriage 101: As a wife, don't ever advise your husband to do this.) Job didn't listen. In fact, Job did not sin even once. He was confused though. Hurting deeply, he asked God something like this: "What on earth are You doing?" But listen to how God responds:

> Where were you when I laid the earth's foundation?
> Tell me, if you understand.
> Who marked off its dimensions? Surely you know!
> Who stretched a measuring line across it?
> On what were its footings set,
> or who laid its cornerstone—
> while the morning stars sang together
> and all the angels shouted for joy? (Job 38:4-7).

Right then, at that moment, Job got it. He remained sinless and proved Satan wrong.

This same God holds the entire world in the palm of His hand. He counts all of the stars and names them too. We are made from dust; He holds stardust in His hands. We think we're smart; He *made* smart. We use words to communicate; He uses words to create.

The best part is that this same God, who ended up blessing Job with twice as much as he had before, is also a very personal God. He loves the world, but He also loves *you*. Though your thoughts are but a mere breath to the Lord of the universe, He notices the tiniest breath you take. Today, breathe deeply and know that as God holds the world in His hands, He is thinking about you.

What's a Girl to Do?

When life is difficult and you're having a hard time understanding what's going on around you, step back for a moment, take a deep breath, and remind yourself how big God really is. Read Psalms. And pray that God will reveal His character to you in the midst of the storm.

Totally Talkin' with God

Father, forgive me when I forget to worship You as I should. Remind me who You are, Lord, and help me to think about Your love, might, and wonder. Bring me back to the true reality: I worship the one true God. Deepen my relationship with You through Jesus Christ. In His name, amen.

Bloom Where You Are Planted

Who knows? Maybe you were made queen for just such a time as this.
ESTHER 4:13 MSG

When I was little, my dad read to me every night. One story I remember in particular is *Beauty and the Beast*. I joined in the story and became a character. It never got old.

As I've gotten older, I find myself loving to read exciting stories, like mystery novels or romantic comedies with cute guys. Fascination takes hold of my heart as I dive into stories with twists, turns, and happy endings.

I am amazed at the many wonderful and adventurous stories in the Bible. Stories about the world around us and how it was created. Stories of family and friendship. Battles won and lost, love and romance, and so much more! One of my favorite Bible stories is the story of Esther, a young girl who became queen. Listen to the story:

King Ahasuerus was looking for a new queen. He got rid of the former queen because she did not do what he wanted her to do. Wow! So his advisors suggested he bring in all the young maidens of Persia, hold a beauty pageant, and pick one. Imagine that!

He chose Esther. The story goes on to say that even though Esther did not want to be queen, she agreed. Esther was an orphan being raised by her cousin, Mordecai, whom she trusted with all her heart. Mordecai was faithful to God and encouraged Esther to stand strong by saying the words in today's focus verse. And you know what? Esther, because she was the queen, was able to save all of her people (the Jews), including herself, from being killed! What strength, courage, and faith she displayed!

Take time today to read the book of Esther. It's short, so you can do it all at once. You will be blessed and encouraged! I am every time I read it. God's fingerprints are clearly evident even though His name is not mentioned in the book. I am always reminded how much He is in control of my life—regardless of the circumstance.

I love the saying "Bloom where you are planted!" Wherever you are in your own life story, remember that God is in control. He wants to use you right where you are. Open your eyes today and see where He wants you to serve. See where He wants you to go. Trust and follow Him, and be ready for the adventure of a lifetime!

What's a Girl to Do?

Think about the people around you, where you often go, and what you do in your daily routine. Pull out your journal or a piece of paper and begin to think of ways you can show the love of Christ to your circle of influence—your Persia—and start blooming today!

Totally Talkin' with God

Father, open my eyes to the world around me—my circle of influence, where You have placed me. Help me see Your purpose for placing me here! May I be used for Your glory always. In Jesus' name, amen.

Me, Me, Me

You ask and do not receive, because you ask with wrong
motives, so that you may spend it on your pleasures.
JAMES 4:3 NASB

Have you ever wondered whether God really hears you when you pray? Or do you pray about something that never seems to get answered—at least not the way you wanted it to? This has happened to me quite often. At times like that, I feel as though God may not even be listening to me. Have you been there?

On the other hand, on some days my relationship with God seems so close. I pray and talk with Him and can see Him working in my life and answering my prayers.

When Jesus prayed in Gethsemane, just prior to being taken captive to be crucified on the cross, He prayed a prayer I think we all would have prayed. He basically said something like this: *Father, if at all possible, please take this cup from Me. I don't want to have to go through this. Is there another way?* I think if we were in Jesus' shoes, we would have stopped our prayer right there. *God, help me get out of this!* Thankfully, Jesus continued: *If there's no other way, I certainly understand. I want to do Your will.*

Jesus had it figured out. He knew that the reason He was on this earth was to live out the Father's will for His life. Therefore, instead of just praying for what He wanted (which He did), He threw another possibility out there: *Yet I will do whatever You want Me to, Father. I am here for You.* Jesus didn't push His own agenda. He did not ask with wrong motives. He prayed not that His will be done, but that His Father's will be done.

Rarely do I hear Christians pray for God's will regardless of the outcome. Why don't we pray like this? I think it's because we're scared to ask for God's will. We fear the outcome. We fear being left to deal with heartache. Or we struggle to believe He has our best interests at heart.

When we get to know other people really well, we see who they are beneath the surface. We see how much they care and love us, and trusting them becomes easier. Even if what is ahead may be scary and undesirable, tackling the problem is easier when we can lean on a relationship built on trust.

Relationships are built on good communication. If we desire to be totally God's, we need to work on communicating with Him—not just telling Him our desires, but also listening for His desires for us. God knows that His will for my life is so much better than my own. When I approach Him in prayer, I have to be convinced that He knows me better than I know myself. Jesus knew this. And He was tremendously close with the Father as a result. I believe their close relationship made it much easier for Jesus to say and truly mean, "I want Your will, Father, not Mine."

Spend time with your heavenly Father today. Ask Him how to trust Him with His will for your life. Then be open to His leading and what He may be showing you!

What's a Girl to Do?

Let's attempt to test ourselves for "selfish" prayers. Listen as you pray. Listen to your heart and ask the Spirit to guide you to pray with right motives—with God's will in mind, not yours.

Totally Talkin' with God

Father, You are awesome, and I desire to know You and Your will for my life better. Daily I make selfish decisions and even pray selfish prayers. Move me to pray in a more humble way. I love You! In Jesus' name, amen.

Overcoming the Hard Times

I have told you these things, so that in me you may have peace. In this
world you will have trouble. But take heart! I have overcome the world.

I love watching my little brother play sports. He is really good. And he
has also been very fortunate to play on a lot of winning teams. His
baseball team finished fifth in the nation when he was just 11 years old.

I, on the other hand, have not been as fortunate. I have been on some
losing teams through the years. The difference, though (and don't tell
Zach I said this), is that he takes losing a little harder than I did.

Losing in sports is one thing. Losing in life is quite another. Maybe
you didn't pass a test even though you studied like crazy for it. Or you
applied for a job but didn't get it, or a relationship didn't work out, or you
didn't make a spot on a team or a choir. Life can be hard on us, but we
don't need to be hard on ourselves. I have come to learn the difference
between losing and being a loser.

On several occasions, Jesus warned His disciples about His impending
death on the cross. (Talk about hard times!) In today's focus verse, we see
Him adding something like this: "I've told you this now so you won't fear,
but rather will have peace. In the world you'll have trouble—no question
about it. But you're in Me, and remember, I've overcome the world."

I looked up the word *overcome* to see what Jesus was referring to. It
means to prevail, conquer, or defeat. When we're going through a difficult time and feel as if we're losing in the game of life, how can we keep
the attitude of a conqueror? It comes by faith (1 John 5:4). Our unshak-
able belief in Jesus gives us the spirit of a war hero so we can prevail and
conquer in His name.

What we conquer, though, is not physical things, but things like sin,
hopelessness, sadness, brokenness, defeat...all of the emotions that tear
us apart. We conquer lies, like the belief that our mistakes make us losers.
You and I *will* mess up sometimes. After all, we're human. Satan sneers
when we degrade ourselves, and he enjoys seeing people hurt us. The

devil loves it when we believe that we are losers, that we're stuck, that we're not good enough.

I know life's not fair. It never will be. But this does not change the most powerful truth: We are already on the side of the true winner. Through Christ, we can prevail over the label *loser*.

Jesus *has* overcome the world. When He chose to come to earth and live as a man (Philippians 2:7-8), never sin (2 Corinthians 5:21), and then die on the cross and rise again so all who believe will live (Colossians 1:20,22), He won. And He didn't just win a gold medal and take a victory lap. He defeated death. And when we are in Him, we win too.

Truth is powerful. The Bible says that in Christ, we can overcome, prevail, and conquer sin, temptation, doubt, addiction, abuse...whatever.

Don't give up on yourself. God hasn't given up on you! And a relationship with Him changes everything!

What's a Girl to Do?

Don't give up. Don't listen to the lies of the world. We are not losers, but winners. The world may not acknowledge that, but that's because the world doesn't want to acknowledge Christ. Be strong and live by faith.

Totally Talkin' with God

Father, I am so thankful that I am in You. You are the winner. I have overcome because I am in You. Thank You for this promise. Help me to live out this truth. In Jesus' name, amen.

Prepare for Battle

Put on the full armor of God, so that you will be able
to stand firm against the schemes of the devil.
EPHESIANS 6:11 NASB

I love to think about the wonderful summer nights I've enjoyed looking at the stars. The moon shines down; friends and family join together to sing, laugh, and tell funny stories around a campfire; and don't forget the s'mores! Ah, the joys of summer.

Sitting peacefully next to the fire, you feel a sudden sting. Then another. You smack your leg. Then your arm. The next thing you know, mosquitoes are everywhere. It's a covert attack! Before long you find yourself dancing around to the music of the mosquitoes, smacking yourself like a loon. I hate bugs!

Mosquitoes are one thing. The spiritual attack we're under is quite another. When I first learned about our spiritual battle, I was scared and excited at the same time. I thought, *Yeah, I'm tough—let's go!* But then I changed my mind. *Wait! I didn't sign up to be a soldier. I'm not in the army. I don't want to fight!* But the truth is, a battle is raging. It's invisible, but it's real.

Be prepared. You're up against far more than you can handle on your own. Take all the help you can get, every weapon God has issued, so that when it's all over but the shouting you'll still be on your feet. Truth, righteousness, peace, faith, and salvation are more than words. Learn to apply them. You'll need them throughout your life. God's Word is an indispensable weapon. In the same way, prayer is essential in this ongoing warfare. Pray hard and long. Pray for your brothers and sisters. Keep your eyes open. Keep each other's spirits up so that no one falls behind or drops out (Ephesians 6:13-18 MSG).

When the apostle Paul wrote those words, he lived in an age that was different from ours. In the twenty-first century, warfare is primarily electronic, not hand-to-hand. We don't carry swords or worry too much about being close to the battlefront. But maybe we should. The front lines are closer than we think.

Fencing classes might be a blast, but I don't think we should all hurry to sign up. I was thinking we should start more Bible studies and prayer groups. The weapons God wants us to use come from a close relationship with Him and fellowship with other believers.

Did you notice in the Scripture above how important prayer is? It's essential to help us during battle. And did you see the emphasis on the Word of God? It's described as an "indispensable weapon." Both are vital to help us be more aware of our enemy and his attacks.

What if we did start Bible studies and prayer groups? Do you think they would make a difference? I do! The Bible describes the devil as a prowling lion ready to devour us (1 Peter 5:8). But we have the victor on our side—Jesus Christ! He has already defeated Satan, and death has no power over those who believe in Jesus. By preparing for battle (reading the Word and praying) we will have success on the battlefield.

Truth, righteousness, peace, faith, and salvation. All of us have full access to this armor. Start training today!

What's a Girl to Do?

You and I should begin to prepare for battle right now. From the instant we wake up in the morning to our final waking moments before we drift off to sleep at night, we are in a spiritual battle. We must prepare and know God's battle plan (it's found in His Word). Begin today to study, prepare, and ask for God's wisdom to discern the enemy's strategy for attacking you.

Totally Talkin' with God

Father, You have provided me with the tools to stand against my enemy. Thank You! I know Satan can use other people to hurt me, but my true enemy is him—the devil. I love You, Lord. Help me be a prepared soldier in the battle that is already raging around me. In Jesus' name, amen.

Amazing Grace

He said to me, "My grace is sufficient for you, for my power is made
perfect in weakness." Therefore I will boast all the more gladly
about my weaknesses, so that Christ's power may rest on me.

2 CORINTHIANS 12:9

Have you ever taken an exam and gotten a really bad grade? (If you're breathing, I'm sure you can say yes. But if the answer is no, we'll see you at Harvard in a few years.) As you stare with horror at the bad grade on your exam, you suddenly hear the teacher or professor say, "I'm going to curve the exam by ten points. Keep working hard."

Party time! You were given a better grade even though you know you didn't deserve it. That's grace! Grace is when you are given something you don't deserve.

And God is full of grace. We haven't earned His love, His protection, or His provision. Yet He still offers these things freely and willingly. And He does so for anyone regardless of whether she meets His standard of being good enough, which is good news because none of us meet that standard anyway.

We know that humans are sinful. Sometimes we see an undeserving person get a break, and we think, *Of all people, why did* she *get that? A lot of other people deserve it more than she does.* But really, none of us deserve the good things God gives us.

The apostle Paul understood God's grace better than most people do:

> So I wouldn't get a big head, I was given the gift of a handicap to keep me in constant touch with my limitations. Satan's angel did his best to get me down; what he in fact did was push me to my knees. No danger then of walking around high and mighty! At first I didn't think of it as a gift, and begged God to remove it. Three times I did that, and then God told me, "My grace is enough; it's all you need. My strength comes into its own in your weakness."

Once I heard that, I was glad to let it happen. I quit focusing on the handicap and began appreciating the gift. It was a case of Christ's strength moving in on my weakness. Now I take limitations in stride, and with good cheer, these limitations that cut me down to size—abuse, accidents, opposition, bad breaks. I just let Christ take over! And so the weaker I get, the stronger I become (2 Corinthians 12:9-10 MSG).

When Jesus said that His grace was sufficient for Paul, He was basically saying that life with hard times *and* His grace was better than life with no hard times at all. My first reaction is, *I'd much rather not have the problems, Jesus.* But the more I think about it, the more I see what Jesus meant. If Paul had no hard times, he would have never understood God's grace the way he did. When I am at my lowest or think I have nothing to offer, that's when God's power is most obvious.

The Bible says we're not to be ashamed of the gospel, for it is the power of God for our salvation (Romans 1:16). We receive this salvation not by works, but by grace (2 Timothy 1:8-10 NASB). So what do we know of grace so far?

- Grace does not involve work.
- It is undeserved—like receiving something for nothing.
- God shows us grace with His love.

Whenever I think about God's grace, I can't help but remember these lines from one of the most popular hymns of all time:

Amazing grace, how sweet the sound
That saved a wretch like me.
I once was lost, but now I'm found,
Was blind but now I see!"

Grace is love that came down from heaven before we ever asked. We didn't deserve it. I love that about God. He gives it anyway because He loves you and me! Make a list of the ways God has given you His grace, and thank Him today for these amazing gifts!

What's a Girl to Do?

Without grace, we'd be on a never-ending trail of tears and heartache. God has given us His love and salvation as gifts. Even with Christ evident in the world, we still see people around us suffering such pain. Let's show grace to others today by sharing the gifts He's given us!

Totally Talkin' with God

Father, I desire to know You more—Your purposes, Your love, and Your grace. I am beginning to see that I should be grateful for all that I have. So thank You, Lord. I love You! In Jesus' name, amen.

Control Freak

In his heart a man plans his course, but the LORD determines his steps.
PROVERBS 16:9

I hate change. I hate letting go most of all. I remember when my boyfriend was leaving town for my senior year. I was faced with this fact about myself—I'm not very good at good-byes. I guess I get pretty attached to anyone or anything that is important to me.

My mom recalls a story from my childhood. I had a puppy named Rio, and my dad would occasionally let him loose. Rio would run away as fast as he could, and I would run after him, crying and screaming until my dad, after a fierce chase, would place him back into my arms.

Are you like me? Do you fear or hate change? I want to share one of my journal entries about being lonely.

> Why is being alone so…lonely? I need to know my boyfriend loves me, and yet I do know it. How is that logical? How does that make sense? I feel like we are beginning this college separation. And just so you know—it's hard!

When I realized how lonely I was after he left for college, I knew I had to turn back to God and give Him His rightful place in my heart. My desperation after a boy left showed the major place he had in my life—the place of priority that God should have and no one or nothing else.

I bet my need to feel in control has something to do with all of this. I don't like the idea of things being completely out of my hands. Can you relate? Thinking about someone else doing everything for me drives me crazy. Brushing our hair, helping us write our names, tying our shoes… as infants and toddlers we needed others to help us with small tasks. When I grew out of that stage, I thought I didn't need any more help. Even from God.

Now that you're older, what things can make you feel out of control? How about questions like these:

- Will the popular crowd like you?
- Will a boy think you're cute?
- Will you make the cut on the team?
- Will that zit on your forehead disappear?
- Will your friend move away?

You know, we girls like to have things our way. We want what we want, when we want it. And we usually want it *now*! Some of us are pretty used to getting our way. We can have some influence on some of the things I listed above, but mostly we have little say about them.

Change happens. The best way to deal with change is to come to the same conclusion I did when my boyfriend left. I realized I needed to turn back to God and give Him His rightful place in my heart.

Regardless of whether you struggle with change, Christ deserves to reign as King in your heart. Allow Him to sit on the throne of your life, and you will find true joy!

What's a Girl to Do?

Change and letting go of control are two difficult topics to tackle. They are complex and can relate to experiences from our childhoods. I pray that each of us can make progress in giving control over to the Lord.

Totally Talkin' with God

Father, help me to give everything to You. You have shown me a glimpse of how much You love me. I trust in You. Give me the strength to place even the little parts of my life into Your skillful hands. I love You! In Jesus' name, amen.

4

FITTING IN

Devotions on standing up for Christ

Mary, Mary, Quite Amazing

Nothing is impossible with God.

LUKE 1:37

Mary the mother of Jesus was probably about 15 years old. Just a teenager who—at least in my imagination—looked rather plain and simple. But even though she may have looked ordinary, she came from royalty. She was a descendent of King David, and she kept herself pure in anticipation of marriage.

With her wedding fast approaching, Mary had a visit from an angel. Yeah—an angel! Think you wouldn't be afraid? I know Mary was. Especially an angel who says, "Greetings, you who are highly favored!"

What? Me? Highly favored?

"The Lord is with you," the angel continued. Now Mary was scared, and the angel evidently sensed her fear. "Do not be afraid, Mary," the angel said, "you have found favor with God. You will give birth to a son, and you are to give him the name Jesus. He will be great and be called the Son of the Most High."

A baby? What? That's impossible. Mary wasn't married, and she hadn't slept with anyone. As a teenager, Mary took on a huge risk. In fact, she technically should have been stoned to death for going along with having God's baby. What a scandal—back in Mary's day, becoming pregnant before marriage was a big no-no.

And Joseph? He may very well have been shamed by his family and society for marrying a girl who was pregnant (everyone assumed by his doing). But by making Mary his wife, Joseph spared her life and helped her give birth to the promised Savior.

Mary and Joseph—a young couple that other people probably looked down on. They willingly, with God's strength, became weak in the eyes of the world—loners, estranged, outcasts. And it was all God's plan.

The Bible shows us that God sometimes asks His followers (including you and me) to do very difficult things. And many times, responding the right way is difficult. But Mary sets the example: "I am the Lord's servant... May it be as you have said."

That doesn't mean that God will give us perfect, pain-free lives. Following Jesus is often quite the opposite of being comfortable. Just look at a lot of other Christians throughout history! All of Jesus' apostles were killed for believing in Jesus (except maybe John).

I pray we will have the attitude that those in the early church had and that those in other parts of the world have—an attitude that counts it a joy to experience hardships for the Lord.

God asks us to be totally available. Totally committed to His cause. Totally His. And when we do that, we can say in all sincerity, *Your will be done, Lord*, and know that He will be with us through it all. *Yes, God, it's your life, not mine.*

What's a Girl to Do?

I pray that we can have the attitude Mary had: "I am the Lord's servant...May it be to me as you have said." Remember that all things are possible with God. We may not be able to change our attitudes on our own, but let's ask for God's help today.

Totally Talkin' with God

Father, I desire to place my life completely in Your hands, just as Mary did. Give me the strength to obey You and trust Your good and perfect will for my life. Regardless of what You ask of me, help me remember that all things are possible with You, Lord. Help me to trust. In Jesus' name, amen.

Walking the Talk

We're Christ's representatives. God uses us to persuade men and
women to drop their differences and enter into God's work of making
things right between them. We're speaking for Christ himself
now: Become friends with God; he's already a friend with you.

2 CORINTHIANS 5:20 MSG

Deep down, most of us want to be noticed somehow and maybe even become famous. Remember Michael Phelps in the 2008 Summer Olympics? I've never heard so many of my friends raving about one athlete before! Michael Phelps became a hero overnight. He won *eight* Olympic gold medals that year! That's more than anybody else in Olympic history! He had already won six gold medals in the 2004 Olympics. No one else has accumulated fourteen gold medals!

But a few months later, America's swim champ was caught smoking marijuana, and he tried to lie about it. One choice, one moment, and this hero's world was turned upside down. Fans were shocked.

I'm not a swimmer, and I'll never be an Olympic athlete. But in a way, Michael Phelps represented me and you. He's an American. We cheered for him. Being famous is cool, but it can be dangerous too. Michael Phelps learned that the hard way.

The viewing audience for the 2008 Olympics was about 3.2 billion people. You think *that's* impressive? God's girl represents something way, way bigger. God's girl represents Jesus Christ Himself!

The Bible says you and I are God's ambassadors. When Jesus went back to heaven, He didn't just say, "Have fun!" No way! Jesus pretty much told His disciples (and us), "Okay, I'm going to be with My Father. And I'm sending My Spirit to be with you. When people look at you, they'll know that I am real." (See Matthew 28:18-20.)

And here's the best part: In God's kingdom, you don't have to be rich or famous. God is looking for girls who are *willing* to follow Him. Girls who will stand up for Him even when that's not the popular thing to do.

God's looking for girls who are so excited about Jesus they just can't help talking about Him everywhere—at school, with friends, at home, at the mall, at the gym. You name it!

A girl who is totally God's is crazy about Him! When other people look at her, they know she's different. God's girl didn't just pray a prayer one time to accept Christ...she *lives* like Christ.

Are you that kind of girl? Do you want to be? I'm amazed that God has entrusted you and me—His girls—with such a valuable message. We get to tell other people about the saving power and freedom found in Jesus Christ alone!

You and I are working for a prize way more valuable than Michael Phelps's gold medals. One day, we get to hear Jesus say, "Well done, good and faithful servant" (Matthew 25:21). "Good job, Megan! I'm proud of you." Coming from God, *that* will make it all worth it.

Gold medals will get tarnished. Money will run out. Friends will eventually slip out of our lives. But when we work to hear God say, "Well done," we cannot lose.

What's a Girl to Do?

Let's pray and ask God to reveal areas of our lives where we don't represent Christ, and then let's pray for change. It will be hard, and we will probably need to ask God for help over and over. But it's worth it!

Totally Talkin' with God

Father, I have misled those around me with my misrepresentation of You. I know now that I have the privilege of giving the world the good news of salvation through faith in Jesus Christ. Provide me with the boldness and strength to do my best, Lord. All glory to You! In Jesus' name, amen.

Fitting In

In him we were also chosen...in order that we...
might be for the praise of his glory.
EPHESIANS 1:11-12

Some things just don't fit in, like a tugboat that doesn't float, a train with square wheels, and a jack-in-the-box whose name is not Jack.

Our need to fit in reminds me of the Christmas special *Rudolph the Red-Nosed Reindeer*. My family still watches it every year! Remember when Rudolph and the little elf that wanted to be a dentist left Santa's workshop and sailed with a rough outdoorsman to the Island of Misfit Toys? On this little island lived a majestic lion with wings and a gold crown. His job was to fly to every nation, gather misfit toys, and give them a temporary home until Santa found them a suitable new one.

Those poor toys weren't like other toys. They just didn't quite fit the mold. And the saddest part about the tugboat, train, and jack-in-the-box whose name wasn't Jack is what they did. They waited. They waited to be wanted. They waited and waited for Santa's sleigh to pick them up and deliver them to some special little children who would love and cherish them.

Isn't that what we all want? To be loved and cherished, to be picked first at recess, to make the team or cheerleading squad or choir? To find a place where we fit in?

I don't use this word often, but I hate being *rejected*. It hurts. We all want to be chosen first, to be well liked, and just to fit in. And when we don't...well, being left out is one of the worst feelings in the world.

But let me tell you something about God: He loves you and has picked you! I know you may not always feel as if this is true, but it is. The Bible says we were chosen in Him for the praise of His glory. Isn't that cool? We were chosen by God to bring Him glory. God says, "I have chosen you and have not rejected you" (Isaiah 41:9).

If you're like me, you're probably thinking, *That sounds great and all, but I don't always feel like God has chosen me. With everything I have done?*

Why would He choose me to bring Him glory? I'm not good enough. I know this feeling. I've been there.

When we feel like misfits, everything and everybody around us seems to have more power and worth than we do. We certainly don't feel as if God would choose misfits to serve Him. Yet He did! Our feelings waver and often aren't a true gauge of reality. The evil one loves to make us feel unwanted. I think Satan uses this cheap tool because he wants us to believe we mean nothing to God or anyone else, to be convinced that we don't fit anywhere and that we're all alone.

The goal of fitting in is an illusion set up by Satan for our fall. Don't step into his trap by thinking we need to fit into anything this world has to offer. Instead, we need to focus on God's glory, not our own. Follow Jesus' example: "If I glorify myself, my glory means nothing" (John 8:54).

What's a Girl to Do?

If we are overly concerned about whether we fit in, we may be focused on ourselves and not on God. Think about the fact that God has chosen us. Remember that this week.

Totally Talkin' with God

Father, I often forget how much You care for me, so I worry too much about whether others like me. I want to remember Your plan, Your decision to choose me to bring You glory. What an awesome task! I don't feel worthy, but that's okay. I know that You will be working through me. I love You! In Jesus' name, amen.

Reputation on the Line

If serving the LORD seems undesirable to you, then choose
for yourselves this day whom you will serve...But as
for me and my household, we will serve the LORD.
JOSHUA 24:15

What kind of girl are you? I know a gorgeous girl who everyone thinks is a good Christian. But if the right people offered her a chance to get drunk or high, she would because she wants to fit in so bad. If a boy pushed her just a little, she would give in and compromise her values.

Why? To be fair, maintaining our values is hard. And in this case, she seems to have no sense of *who she is* because her decisions are based on how she wants others to see her. She longs to fit in and to be liked. We all do.

I know another girl who's brilliant, but she has made some destructive decisions. This girl is smart, like top-ten-of-her-class intelligent. Her family is very involved in church. She is a lot of fun and nice to everybody. She had a great reputation for being godly and leading others closer to the Lord, but then she got involved in sex, drinking, and partying. Pretty soon the entire school knew about it. It ruined her reputation. She gave in to the pressure and is now making choices that will forever haunt her.

Your reputation is probably one of the hardest things to ever get back. We all want to fit in of course, but sometimes doing the right thing means standing out and doing what everyone else isn't doing. It can mean saying no to what your friends are doing because you know it's wrong. A girl who is totally God's knows who she is, and being popular doesn't matter to her as much as some other things do.

As I look at my friends at school, I realize that some people make choices on their own, but more people make choices based on what other people think. They are followers, not leaders.

Joshua was a leader. He laid it all on the table for the Israelites. He tells God's people that they don't have to serve God. Is that surprising to you? Joshua told the Israelites that obeying God was *their* choice.

Did the people of God turn away? A lot of times they did—but not this time. They chose to serve the Lord (Joshua 24:16,18).

Sure, I want people to like me. But even more, I want to please God. If I compromise what I believe and what I stand for just because I want others to accept me, I'll sacrifice all that I am in the Lord.

It's our choice. God wants us to keep our reputations pure as a witness to Him—not because He's a killjoy but because He wants what is best for us and wants to include us in His plans for the world. God loves us more than we could imagine, and He knows that when we live to fit in, we only end up with deep wounds and hurt feelings.

Jesus treasures your heart...do you?

What's a Girl to Do?

I don't want to follow the crowd; I want to lead. I want God to be happy with my decisions even if my peers aren't. And I want you to do the same. Together, let's take this challenge to maintain pure reputations. God will help us do it.

Totally Talkin' with God

Father, You have revealed Your character to me in the Bible and in everyday life. You listen when I pray and answer my prayers as You see best. I know You are real, and I know You hate sin. Help me to live purely for You and no one else. In Jesus' name, amen.

Stand Out

I am not seeking glory for myself; but there is
one who seeks it, and he is the judge.
JOHN 8:50

My junior year in high school was one of the most amazing times in my life. I was chosen to be one of five candidates on my school's Winterfest court. The day before the crowning, each contestant delivered a challenge to the student body. I'll never forget the night I prepared my speech.

I cuddled up with my mom on the couch, and we started talking about God's dreams for our lives, about God's plans and our desires, about His love and our mistakes.

"Mom," I asked her, "why do we try so hard to fit in when God created us to stand out?"

As we fumbled around trying to answer the question, I began to realize the ways I strive to fit in. I felt a little sheepish, especially when my mom quoted Jesus. The least she could do was quote somebody I could disagree with!

My mom said that Jesus knew He was meant to stand out, and that helped Him to never back down when others rejected or opposed Him. He was so bold that the Jews picked up stones one time and were ready to kill Him right there in the temple. But Jesus didn't let other people define Him.

Judy Garland once said, "Always be a first-rate version of yourself instead of a second-rate version of somebody else." Jesus wasn't going to pretend He was somebody else in order to please the crowd. He lived to bring glory to His Father, not to Himself.

The Father never intended for Jesus to fit in. And He doesn't want you to either. Imagine for a moment what people look like when they try to fit in. They may wear the trendy clothes, show athletic promise, drink alcohol, do drugs, and sleep around. Basically, those who want to be "in" do whatever everyone else does. This makes me wonder, how does that make them unique?

Max Lucado wrote *If I Only Had a Green Nose*, a book about standing out and about being fashionable. Punchinello, the main character, realizes that he doesn't fit in, so he and his friends follow the trend and paint their noses green.

In the end, Punchinello and his friends can't keep up with the constant change in nose color trends. "We just want to be ourselves again," said Punchinello's friend, Splint.

"I'm glad to hear that," said Eli (aka God).

"Can we?" they asked.

"Of course you can," Eli replied. "I'll always help you to be who I made you to be." Eli proceeded to sand off the paint on the wooden Wemmicks' noses. It was painful, but they were happy to be themselves again.

We were made to be unique. We were not made to fit in. God's girl values herself far more than that. You and I were made to stand out for Jesus.

What's a Girl to Do?

Take action to stop fitting in and begin standing out. Ask God to reveal the ways you try hard to conform to others. Then ask Him to empower you to stop. Begin to love the you He has made, the you that is meant to stand out!

Totally Talkin' with God

Father, You took the time to form me even before I was born. You made me unique and special—different from any other human. Forgive me when I try to be like others. Strengthen my resolve to live like no one but who You made me to be—a follower of Jesus. I love You! In Jesus' name, amen.

Be Bold

Light, space, zest—that's God! So, with him on my
side I'm fearless, afraid of no one and nothing.
PSALM 27:1 MSG

Giving my speech for the Winterfest court was one of the scariest things I've ever done, but it taught me to be bold. Here's what I wrote in my journal:

> Today was one of the most amazing days of my life! I gave my speech today as a Winterfest candidate, and I watched Christ work through my life! It was amazing! Incredible! Exhilarating! It doesn't even matter who wins because I believe God allowed me to do this to show me I am capable of public speaking. The thing that touched me most was how many people told me they voted for me—not because they did, but why they did. I want my testimony to shine before everyone! I love You, Lord! I am Yours now and forever! Thank You for blessing me today.

As I go back and read my thoughts from the past, I can almost feel the excitement again. God truly met me that day and displayed through my weakness a power I didn't even know existed. I stood in front of a crowd of my peers and made myself completely vulnerable. In my state of fear, God became my strength.

Why are we so afraid? Perhaps we don't want to make the wrong choice and get in trouble. We don't want to look bad in front of our friends, or we worry too much about what others think about us. We worry that others might see our flaws.

The Bible uses many images to describe Jesus. Here are two: light (John 1:9) and truth (John 14:6). Think about this. When you are in the light, you can't hide anything. The light reveals what's in us—the beautiful and the ugly. It brings out the truth. Nothing can be hidden when we are fully exposed.

Scripture tells us that Christ is both light and truth. We don't need to be afraid to come into the light. We may see things we'd rather not see, but those will be the things that are not filled with the truth, like sinful habits we have yet to give up. Lies we have believed about God and the world. Lies we have believed about ourselves.

There is no real formula, but get this: When we are weak (2 Corinthians 12:8,10), we come into the light, and God can fill us with His strength. The light reveals the truth. No stone is left unturned. And the truth (Jesus) sets us free (John 8:32). No more bondage to sin—we are free in Christ.

Don't fear the light. Run from the darkness and into the light. Embrace the truth and live freely.

What's a Girl to Do?

We all can benefit from a good dose of humility in the Lord. With God on our side, we have nothing to fear. Today, do something for God you normally would be afraid to do. For example, maybe you could tell someone about Jesus.

Totally Talkin' with God

Father, living in fear is no fun. It makes me look bad, it's uncomfortable, and it can be painful. When I do act for You even though I am afraid, You always give me strength. I pray that as I come into the light, I will encourage others to come into the light as well. Help me be in the light, Lord. In Jesus' name, amen.

Respect Yourself

If any of you lacks wisdom, let him ask of God, who gives to all
generously and without reproach, and it will be given to him.
JAMES 1:5 NASB

R-E-S-P-E-C-T. Girl, you and I were created in the image of God. He wants us to respect ourselves—and other people too.

What does respect look like? When my boyfriend flirted with a pretty girl he hung out with on occasion, I was hurt. I cried. I didn't want to say anything, but I knew I couldn't be little Megan who sweeps everything under the rug. I had to respect myself.

I had to realize that I was worth standing up for. I needed to confront my boyfriend's actions. This wasn't a life-and-death experience. It wasn't even a huge drama. But when God showed me I am worth respecting, I learned to not be afraid to confront others when they hurt me.

My dad always has great advice about dealing with guys. He is so wise! I'll never forget him telling me, "Megan, you are who you spend time with." Here are a few other things I've learned:

- *We are 100 percent responsible for our walk with God.* If you feel distance between you and the Lord, guess who moved. Why does God sometimes feel distant? Because I chose not to call to Him in prayer. Why don't I feel like I know Him? Because I chose not to read His Word. Draw near to Him, and He'll draw near to you (James 4:8).

- *Make decisions based on the Word of God.* Make an effort to read the Word and pray every day. These things will change your life, and the decisions you make will no longer be as complicated as you might think.

- *The choices you make depend a lot on who you hang with.* You will be a leader or a follower. Decide who you are and whom you will associate with. Spend time with those who challenge you and build you up in Christ.

- *Don't fear failure.* I have good news and bad news. The bad news is, you will fail. The good news is, failure won't cripple you if you don't let it. Trust God and take a step.

- *Choose to compliment people.* And be sincere about it. When you serve others, you'll feel better, you'll get to know them better, and you'll be less likely to be obsessed with yourself.

- *Respect yourself.* Don't let important things slide, as I was tempted to do with my boyfriend issue. You are valuable! Know who you are in Christ and make decisions based on that truth.

Remember, the important thing is not what everyone else thinks about you, but what God thinks about you. You are who the Lord says you are. Lean on the truths you find in the Bible, and go ahead and sweep the rest under the rug.

What's a Girl to Do?

Self-respect comes easier for some than for others. For me, it doesn't come naturally. Challenge yourself this week to respect yourself in new ways.

Totally Talkin' with God

Father, thank You for who You are and all You share with me. I pray that You will give me wisdom to respect myself. You have made me to be loved, not kicked around. Help me to reach out to others who struggle to embrace the people You have made them to be. I want to encourage them to look to You for their true identity. In Jesus' name, amen.

Conflict

If it is possible, as far as it depends on you, live at peace with everyone.
ROMANS 12:18

He said, she said, they said...whom do we believe? Do we dare question? That might cause an argument—not fun.

You and I are human. Because we're human, we will have conflicts. They are inevitable. But let me tell you, conflict does *not* have to mean drama. Think of major blowup with a friend that you worked through together. After you worked it out, didn't you feel closer?

People say, "Absence makes the heart grow fonder." Well, replace the word *absence* with *conflict*. It's true. A good fight with a healthy resolution can actually make you and your friend tighter than ever before.

Conflict can bring us to new stages in our relationships. It builds intimacy. Sometimes we need to go through the fire before we can forge a stronger bond. The same applies to our relationship with God. Christians who have been persecuted, lost loved ones, or suffered serious pain in life often say their trials brought them closer to Jesus.

I know I've talked a lot about relationships, but that's because I believe they're the most important things in life. They are what God created us for—to be in relationship with Him and each other.

Daydreaming at school, what do your thoughts wander to? Lying in bed at night, what do you worry about? What distracts you from doing your homework? Why is your phone buzzing with texts? It's all about relationships—with boyfriends, Mom, Dad, best friends, roommates, coworkers, grandparents, siblings, classmates...

We love relationships, but we despise conflict. Yet we can hardly have one without the other. In his book *Everybody's Normal Till You Get to Know Them*, John Ortberg, a really great pastor and writer, gives some wonderful help on resolving conflict:

- Acknowledge the problem.
- Take responsibility for your part in the conflict.

- Take action. Go to the person and sit with her, one-on-one, alone.

Rather than holding the hurt inside, Pastor Ortberg says we need to *talk* about it. Describe what you experienced and observed, how you felt, and the consequences you suffered. Then request that a change take place.

Life's too short to live with hurt between you and a friend. Whether your problem is with your parents, friends, boyfriend, or someone else, make sure you seek reconciliation (forgiveness and healing). And if you have hurt somebody else, go to him or her and offer your apologies. I know it's humbling and not at all easy, but you'll be glad you did.

When we get to heaven, God isn't likely to care much about whether we got an A or B on a science test. I do believe He will care about the people we've influenced during our time on earth.

Are you a real friend? If not, it's never too late to start. "Faithful are the wounds of a friend" (Proverbs 27:6 NASB).

What's a Girl to Do?

Conflict and fighting come with relationships. The trick is to handle these things kindly and with love. Pray that God will keep you from becoming nasty and mean. If you are currently in a conflict, take the advice you just read about. Go and make amends. Peace is worth the price.

Totally Talkin' with God

Father, You desire that relationships be restored. That is why You sent Jesus— so that we may be reconciled to You. Help me to restore hurting relationships. Give me Your wisdom, and let Your peace rest on those whom I need to ask to forgive me. I love You, Lord. In Jesus' name, amen.

5

WHEN LIFE'S NOT FAIR

Devotions for when life keeps pushing us down

Forgiveness

Then Jesus said to her, "Your sins are forgiven."

LUKE 7:48

Have you seen the Christmas movie *Elf*? It's a super funny comedy about a baby named Buddy who slips into Santa's pack at an orphanage, gets transported to the North Pole, and is raised by elves. Yet he doesn't quite fit in. He breaks toys and works much slower than the real elves. But Buddy has a pure heart, and he sets out to find his real father.

Throughout the movie, a theme is forgiveness. Buddy forgives his father for abandoning him. Later, his dad forgives him for creating chaos at his dad's job.

Stories of forgiveness are all through the Bible too. My favorite occurs at a dinner in the house of a Pharisee. While Jesus is at the table, a sinful woman brings in an alabaster jar of perfume. She stands behind Jesus, wets His feet with her tears, and wipes the dampness away with her hair. She kisses His feet and anoints them with the perfume. Simon, the Pharisee who had invited Jesus to dine with him, comments that if Jesus were a prophet, He would know what kind of a woman (likely a prostitute) touched Him. (See Luke 7:36-39.)

Jesus replies with this: "Simon, I have something to say to you. A man loaned money to two people. One he gave five hundred denarii, and the other fifty. Neither had paid him back. He decides that it's no big deal and forgives them both. Which guy do you think will love the money lender more?"

Simon answers, "The guy who had the bigger debt forgiven."

Jesus agrees. Then He turns to the woman but continues talking to Simon. "That's why she loves me so much—because she has been forgiven so much. But the one who is forgiven little, loves little."

Forgiveness is powerful! I want to be like this woman. I have been forgiven much. I want to love much in return.

Jesus didn't wait until we were good enough before He died on the cross. He gave up His life for us while we were yet sinners (Romans 5:8).

85

If somebody has wronged you and has never sought forgiveness, that doesn't mean you should carry unforgiveness around with you. Forgiving someone releases the pressure from you. It doesn't mean you forget about what she did or pretend that she didn't hurt you. It means you decide not to let it weigh you down any longer.

I realize you are likely to have deep, deep wounds. People may have abused you, and you may not be able to even imagine forgiving them. That will be a process between you and God because He understands your pain (Hebrews 4:15). He was beaten, hated, and killed. He was kicked, spat upon, and called names, all for the sake of His love for us.

Before we can forgive, we must first accept God's forgiveness. Ask God to set your heart free to forgive! Let go of any bitterness you are holding. Learn to release the pain and accept God's love, forgiveness, and healing today!

What's a Girl to Do?

This is a hard topic but an important one. Forgiving those who hurt us can only bring us closer to God. Pray that God will remind you of any people who have hurt you or whom you have hurt. Then ask God to help you truly forgive them or ask for their forgiveness. I promise, the experience will be awesome and freeing.

Totally Talkin' with God

Father, I know I have hurt others, and I have a list of others who have hurt me. I can't hide it. You know my heart, Lord. Give me the strength to go to those I have hurt and ask for forgiveness, and help me to truly forgive those who have hurt me. In Jesus' name, amen.

Remolded

O LORD, you are our Father. We are the clay, you are
the potter; we are all the work of your hand.
ISAIAH 64:8

Did you ever make one of those clay pots in elementary school? One
that looked *really* bad but that your mom loved? My mom still has
mine—the pot only a mother could love. She now keeps her coins in it.

For potters who make real clay pots, however, the final masterpiece
is not as easy to create as it was in your third-grade art class. The potter
uses his hands to guide the clay as it spins on a wheel, slowly making
sure the clay does not become too thin or too thick. If he is not happy
with the sculpture he created, he smashes the clay into a round ball and
starts all over again. It must take a lot of patience to be a potter!

God sent Jeremiah to a potter's house to receive a word for Israel.
When he arrived, he saw the potter working with clay on the wheel. The
object didn't turn out the way the potter wanted it to, so he remade it
into another creation. Then God said to Jeremiah, "Can I not do with you
as this potter does?" (Jeremiah 18:6).

To be honest, being a girl isn't easy. Every day I hear girls say things
like "I hate my life...my parents are unfair...my hair is flat...my hips are
too big..." and on and on.

You may have good reason to want to change your life. You may have
been seriously hurt because your parents divorced, or you were abused,
or you suffered from health issues or an addiction. Don't be discouraged.
God is the potter; He may remake your situation, or He may take you
through the pain to make you stronger. Whatever God does, He does for
your own good because He loves you.

I admit I really don't want Him to smash my life and start again. But I
want to always say, "If it pleases You to do so, then so be it." As our focus
verse states, "We are the clay, you are the potter; we are all the work of
your hand." How beautiful!

Even though thousands of years have passed, we can still see the image of the potter and the clay clearly. The Potter's lesson for us transcends time—we are clay in His hands. As you think about your life, remember that it is moldable. Every situation is an opportunity for growth. Be teachable and willing to be molded.

What's a Girl to Do?

Write down a list of all your good qualities. If you can't think of any, ask someone who cares about you to help you list the wonderful things about yourself. Then, take that list and pray in thanksgiving to the Potter for the way He has chosen to create you.

Totally Talkin' with God

Father, I'm sorry. I often mistreat myself. I put myself down and say bad things about the way You have chosen to mold me. I may want to be different, but the way You have made me is pleasing to You. And if it is not, change me, Lord. In Jesus' name, amen.

Words Can Hurt

The tongue is a fire, the very world of iniquity; the tongue is set
among our members as that which defiles the entire body, and
sets on fire the course of our life, and is set on fire by hell.

JAMES 3:6 NASB

S ticks and stones may break my bones, but words will never hurt me."
My friends and I stood at the top of the biggest slide on the playground
and yelled these words to the guys who were bullies in our class.

Whoever made up that saying must have been crazy! What was she
thinking? Words do hurt—terribly! Words can often cause much deeper
wounds than hands, although injuries from either can be horrible.

You may have endured verbal abuse from those who were supposed to
love you. This is wrong, and it breaks my heart. I even want to say mean
things in return to those who have hurt you in order to make everything
right—but it wouldn't.

Our tongues can be the most unruly part of our bodies. If we don't
keep our tongues in check, we can hurt others and ourselves, leaving
deep scars for life.

All of us have said things we regret. Maybe you've had an opportunity
to apologize and ask for forgiveness. But you may not have been given
such an opportunity, or if you have, you just might not be ready.

Sometimes, when others choose to hurt us, our view of God changes.
We have a hard time imagining anyone, including our heavenly Father,
saying kind things about us. But take a look at what God has done for
you and me:

- The Creator of the world took the time to create us (Genesis
  1:27);
- He pieced us together in our mother's womb and marked our
  days (Psalm 139:15-16);
- and He loved us enough to send His only Son, that whoever
  believes in Him will not perish, but have eternal life (John
  3:16).

God loves you and has a wonderful plan for your life. That wonderful plan is for you to trust in Jesus and live for Him.

I pray that no amount of bad words can hurt you enough to make you forget how much God cares for you. Ask God for His strength to forgive those who have caused you pain. Strive to be the kind of girl who uses her words to uplift and encourage—not tear down. Begin today!

What's a Girl to Do?

Let's closely watch what words come out of our mouths. We might be pretty convicted by what we hear. Then let's change for the better. Even if we have to keep our mouth shut or walk away from a group, let's do it. It is worth the small amount of persecution to do as God directs and keep our tongues in check.

Totally Talkin' with God

Father, forgive me when I allow my mouth to ramble. And help me to forgive others who have said things that have hurt me. I long to focus on how much You love me, Lord. May that be my peace and saving grace in times of hurt or temptation. In Jesus' name, amen.

Unconditional Love

But God demonstrates His own love toward us, in that
while we were yet sinners, Christ died for us.
ROMANS 5:8 NASB

Have you ever done something bad? If you said no, you're lying, and...
well, now you've done something bad!

We all have a story or two for which we feel awful—so awful that we
may even think we don't deserve to be forgiven. We may begin to think
that when others mistreat us, we had it coming. Many of us go as far as
believing we shouldn't live.

Or the opposite can happen. Instead of taking responsibility for our
own bad decisions, we pass the blame on to others and point fingers. We
say things like "*You* should have..." instead of "*I* should have..."

Which way is the right way to respond in hard times? Of course, both
contain unhealthy viewpoints, and neither is correct.

God's love is huge, deep, and unconditional—it's called *agape* love.
Most of us know people who love us regardless of the stupid things we
say and do. They might be our parents, grandparents, siblings, or good
friends. We trust that even if we did something terrible, they would
never leave us.

But here's the great news! God is a Rock, a firm foundation on which
we can always depend (Psalm 31:2-3). He did break once—when He chose
to die on the cross for our sins. But then He rose again from the grave.
A winner! Unbroken. Complete. Ready to forgive our sins when we put
our faith and trust in Him—for eternity!

Learn to lean on the Rock! He will not break, disappoint you, or let
you down. His love never fails. Trust Him always!

What's a Girl to Do?

Where do you usually lay your burdens? Where do you place your
confidence and hope? Ask God about this, and be ready for the answer.

Acknowledging the truth and changing may be difficult, but the best way is to hope only in Jesus.

Totally Talkin' with God

Father, I know in my heart that You are truly the only one who will not let me down. I also know I will probably still have to face bad things. I know I may sin, but I'm so glad You will always be there. Guide me into a closer relationship with Jesus. Help me to lean on You without a second thought. In Jesus' name, amen.

Hard Times

Blessed are you when people insult you, persecute you and
falsely say all kinds of evil against you because of me. Rejoice
and be glad, because great is your reward in heaven.
MATTHEW 5:11-12

The *Hiding Place* by Corrie ten Boom is a famous book about leaning on Jesus during hard times. If you haven't read it, you should! It's a classic. Corrie retells her tale from WWII, when her family began to hide Jews in their home. A man who specialized in creating hiding places visited their house and found a perfect place. Corrie started an elaborate system to feed, house, and protect Jewish citizens from the Nazi army.

Until they were caught.

Corrie, her elderly father, her sister, and others were taken to a horrible concentration camp that we still hear about today. Her family died, but God sustained Corrie's life. Eventually, she saw her freedom when the war ended. After that, Corrie traveled, telling her story of forgiveness until her death. Her legacy still lives on.

American Christians deal with hardships, but we aren't usually persecuted physically. You and I are among the richest people in the world... even if we don't have the newest and latest iPod.

Our battle may not be to endure physical torture. Our battlefields are more likely to be the mind and heart. Satan constantly lies to us and entices us to exchange the riches of God's kingdom for personal pleasure. And it's a hard fight!

Corrie always taught Christians to be prepared. When she spoke, she encouraged believers to be ready. Here's her list of necessities:

- Feed on the Word. Digest it. Be involved in a disciplined Bible study.

- Develop a personal relationship with Christ. Not just a casual friendship, but an intimate walk with the Lord.

- Be filled with the Holy Spirit. We Christians are given the Spirit when we believe in Jesus Christ, but we don't always allow the Spirit to work through us.
- Be ready to help others and encourage them. When we are weak, that's actually when we are strong. Be there for your brothers and sisters in Christ.
- Cultivate the fruit of the Spirit (Galatians 5:22-23).

What do you think? Does it make you want to gear up, or would you rather run and hide?

I'm not trying to scare you, but the truth is, hard times will come. You may have already experienced a terribly hard situation—the loss of a family member, homelessness, unjust treatment, or something else.

I want to end with this encouragement: Regardless of what comes your way, do not fear. God is with you (Isaiah 41:10). Be prepared for battle. Engage and fight. Go in God's strength and believe His promise—you are completely in His hands!

What's a Girl to Do?

We can prepare for difficult situations by walking closely with the Lord as Corrie suggests. She studied and gathered her ideas from Scripture and her own experience. This may sound hard, but don't be afraid. God will uphold us in His righteous right hand (Isaiah 41:10).

Totally Talkin' with God

Father, You are in control and above all. I know You love me and want only Your good and perfect will in my life. I ask You to help me in my preparations. I can't do anything without Your help, Lord. I trust and rely on You always. In Jesus' name, amen.

Even Steven

For we know Him who said, "VENGEANCE IS MINE, I WILL
REPAY." And again, "THE LORD WILL JUDGE HIS PEOPLE."
HEBREWS 10:30 NASB

Have you ever wanted to get back at someone who hurt you? How about a friend who stabbed you in the back or an ex-boyfriend who started a vicious rumor? Or how about a sister who took your best shirt without asking and then ruined it? I know I have wanted revenge—bad. Who hasn't? And I hate to say it, but getting even feels good at times.

But Jesus said that if we judge others, we ourselves will be judged. How would you feel if you found out your friends had been discussing something you said or did, and they labeled you falsely? You'd probably feel betrayed, hurt, angry. That's the price of judgment. And if we so easily judge others, we will just as easily receive their judgment.

Okay, so we don't want to get revenge, and we try to reject negative thoughts about our friends. Is that enough? If we choose to hang around people who judge others, don't think for a moment they don't judge us when we're not around. Why wouldn't they? They do everyone else. Do we want to be that way? Do we want friends like them? No way!

Before I say any more, if you know you have hurt someone by judging her, go apologize. Your heart will be healed by such a small, humble act. God desires for you to seek peace with others, and you will be blessed when you obey Him.

When you have been wronged, the emotions you feel are real. Your heart aches and your soul screams when you are hurt. These feelings need to be addressed. You need to communicate how you feel in a gentle and calm way. Clear the air and keep your good relationships healthy.

The Lord will take care of those who hurt us. Our hope, though, should be for their hearts to turn to the Lord—not for fire to fall down from heaven and consume them. Jesus tells us to love our enemies and pray for those who persecute us (Matthew 5:44).

It's not easy, but God will guide your steps and give you the strength you need!

What's a Girl to Do?

Even if we want to get even, we shouldn't. Revenge will not bring glory to God, and we may lose the witness we have in Christ. Sure, we may regain that eventually, but why risk it in the first place? God does such a better job of settling accounts. Let's leave that to Him.

Totally Talkin' with God

Father, I can so easily be stirred to anger and vengeance when people hurt me. Help me to forgive them, ask forgiveness from the ones I've hurt, and look to You for comfort. Take care of me, Lord. In Jesus' name, amen.

I'm Just...Feeling Down

*I am weary with my sighing; every night I make my bed swim, I
dissolve my couch with my tears. My eye has wasted away
with grief; it has become old because of all my adversaries.*
PSALM 6:6-7 NASB

Once upon a time, there was a man who faced a lot of disappointments. His children wouldn't listen to him, other people attacked him, and he struggled with his own sins. Finally, he was in distress and full of depression.

But this man was also the most popular king in the history of the Jewish people—King David. You'd never know he was such a popular and successful king if you read some of his stories.

Depression is a huge problem among American teens. Statistics from www.teendepression.org show these staggering figures:

- About 20 percent of teens will experience depression before they reach adulthood.

- Between 10 and 15 percent of teenagers have some symptoms of depression at any one time.

- About 5 percent of teens are suffering from major depression at any one time.

Depression can affect you regardless of your gender, social background, income level, race, or school setting, though teenage girls report suffering from depression more often than boys. Here are some steps you can take to prevent depression or find your way out:

- Avoid alcohol or drugs because these can trigger depression.
- Associate with positive friends.
- Learn healthy ways to deal with stress.
- Eat a healthy, well-balanced diet.
- Exercise can manage stress and fight depression.

- Consider keeping a journal.
- When you are hurt, allow yourself to grieve for a normal period of time. If your strong feelings of grief last longer, seek counseling.

Each of us has experienced pain and heartache. We may struggle with a serious problem that makes us sad. Maybe we have a family history of depression or a personal long-term illness or disability. We could experience a big trauma or loss, or we might struggle with everyday difficulties at home, at school, or with friends. If you can relate to any of those things, you're not alone.

I've had depressed feelings, and I know how unpleasant they can be. If you struggle with feeling down for a long period of time, please don't hesitate to contact a Christian counselor who can help. Tackle the issue early because young women who don't deal with their depression can develop substance abuse problems, education and career setbacks, and relationship strains. Of course, if the depression lasts too long, it can lead to suicide.

If you aren't depressed but know someone who is, you can help. Here's how:

- Talk to the person and listen.
- Encourage her to be involved in positive activities and take good care of her body.
- Set a good example by taking good care of your body and getting help if you feel depressed or overwhelmed.
- Encourage her to get help.

I realize this devotion has been packed full of statistics and information. Teen depression is not something to take lightly. We need to be proactive to beat this, and King David gave us the perfect first step—take refuge and seek comfort in the Lord. He is your shelter and strong tower! He will see you through.

What's a Girl to Do?

Depression is not something to take lightly. If you are depressed, seek help from God and from a professional counselor. Trust that God will guide you out of the shadows of your thoughts. He is more willing and able than you can imagine!

Totally Talkin' with God

Father, You know my heart. You know my struggles. You know what weighs me down. Enable me to hand over my stress. Guide me to the help I need, Lord. I trust that You are always with me and will never leave me. In Jesus' name, amen.

I Just Need Rest

Come to me, all you who are weary and burdened, and I will
give you rest. Take my yoke upon you and learn from me, for
I am gentle and humble in heart, and you will find rest for
your souls. For my yoke is easy and my burden is light.
MATTHEW 11:28-30

When I was little and got too tired to walk, my dad carried me. He gave me piggyback rides, sat me on his hip, or laid me against his shoulder—anything to get me off my feet. Sometimes Dad cradled me, and my head rested easy because I trusted he wouldn't let go.

I can't tell you how often I wish someone would carry me again!

Have you ever felt as if you needed to be carried through a difficult situation? Hard times are easy to come by. At our age, we can't really rely on our parents to carry us anymore. And our friends don't have the strength to sustain us indefinitely. The only one who can really help us anytime, without failing, for as long as we need is Jesus.

In today's focus verse, Jesus invites us into His arms. He asks us to come and walk with Him. He assures us we will be sustained. And He encourages us that if we bear with Him (wear His yoke), we will see that He is gentle and humble at heart. We will learn from Him and find rest for our souls.

When one of my best friends was in a serious car accident, I leaned on Jesus more than ever. In hindsight, I know He carried me through. I know He did the same for her and her family as well.

When you read our focus verse, you may have wondered what a yoke is. If you have ever seen old pictures or paintings of farm scenes, you may recall the ox or cattle wearing a large, heavy object around their necks. That's the yoke. Ropes were tied to it, and the ropes led to the driver, who tugged this way and that to instruct and guide the animals.

Personally, I think a yoke sounds terrible. But if I have to wear one, I don't want it to be from the world. Why? Well, the world and Jesus are at opposite ends of the spectrum, so the world's yoke would be the opposite of Jesus'. Instead of being gentle, it would be harsh. Instead of being humble, it would be full of pride. Instead of restful, tiresome. Instead of easy, hard. And instead of light, heavy.

When I look at it that way, I want to run to Jesus' side, throw off my worldly yoke, and grab His. I want to find rest in Jesus, and you can too. His arms are open wide—waiting for you!

What's a Girl to Do?

Each of us has burdens to carry. And our worldly yoke is not as nice as the one Jesus offers. We feel overloaded. Some days we can't bear to take another step. Don't wait another second—run into the arms of our Lord and Savior Jesus Christ. He will give you rest.

Totally Talkin' with God

Father, You do all the work. You bore my sins on the cross, died, rose again, and ascended to heaven, where You are preparing a place for me. You will encourage me with Your Spirit until the day You return. And now I find out that You want to give me rest from my burdens—amazing! Thank You, Lord. Help me to take on Your gentle, humble yoke. In Jesus' name, amen.

6

RELATIONSHIPS: BFF'S AND FAMILY

Devotions on the messiness and blessings of friends, family, and other relationships

Confirm or Ignore

Two are better than one, because they have a good return for
their work: If one falls down, his friend can help him up. But
pity the man who falls and has no one to help him up!
ECCLESIASTES 4:9-10

You sit down to your computer, and there it is. The question you love to answer: "Confirm friend request" or "Ignore request"? You guessed it—Facebook.

Here's how it works: During the week, you check your e-mail and see that someone has asked you to be her friend. You follow the link provided, which takes you to your personal Facebook page. Logging on, you either confirm or ignore the request. It's that simple.

But is it?

Having tons of friends feels great, whether on Facebook or in real life. But what happens if your friend request is never confirmed? How does that make you feel? What if that request has been ignored? Sometimes, a simple situation like this can trigger strong emotions—perhaps feelings of rejection, sadness, and confusion.

This devotional is not about the pros and cons of Facebook. Programs like this that connect friends are just a small example of how important and powerful relationships are in our lives—especially for girls! I've heard my dad say, "We are broken in relationships, and we are healed in relationships." Other people hurt us, but we also experience healing with their help and support.

Even with the technology we have at our fingertips now and the power to be connected to other people with the touch of a button, we seem to be more disconnected than ever. We are finding new ways to communicate quickly but with less personal interaction. People rarely visit each other, handwrite a letter, or make a personal phone call.

I love texting. It's super handy and easy. But I wonder how much more of an impact I could have on someone's day if I chose to encourage her in person. For example, if my friend is in the hospital, she may enjoy a personal visit, not just a quick text. Or if my mom's having a bad day, I may want to handwrite a letter or give her a hug, not just an e-card.

You *are* being thoughtful toward others if you text or send e-cards. It's not really about what we do as much as it is about our attitude. It's about genuinely considering other people's needs before our own. Take a moment to think about the best ways to let your family and friends know you love them.

Loving, unselfish behavior toward others shows we care. God encourages us to spread His love near and far. Strengthen your connection to the people who matter to you the most. Be there physically for them and not just through the airways. Take the time—you will be glad you did!

What's a Girl to Do?

Being totally God's includes thinking of others first—being His hands and feet in the lives of those around us. Starting today, make decisions based on investing in what matters most—the relationships God has given you. Take time to show you truly care in a personal way.

Totally Talkin' with God

Father, thank You for loving me the way You do. It's amazing. I want to put You and others before myself. I love You. In Jesus' name, amen.

Training Ground

Our fathers disciplined us for a little while as they thought best; but
God disciplines us for our good, that we may share in his holiness.
HEBREWS 12:10

I used to hate realizing my parents were right, especially when they let me know it.

God has given parents a massive task of raising their children. And discipline is a big part of their responsibilities. I hated being grounded or restricted from going out with friends, but deep down, I knew they cared. The fact is, if our parents never disciplined us, we would have trouble getting through life.

We'll always be under other people's authority—school principals, teachers, professors, police, speed limits (ugh), bosses... You get the picture. Our parents' discipline trains us to obey authority, especially God's authority.

Hebrews 12:10 reminds us that our parents discipline us for this short time on earth as best they know how. When we become adults and are no longer under their supervision, we are able to live in the world on our own. Yet we are still expected to obey civic laws and God's laws.

This verse also says that God will discipline His children. God's discipline may seem scary, but He uses it for our good. He wants us to look and act like Jesus and become holy like Him (1 Peter 1:16). He doesn't want to control us—not at all. Rather, He loves us and wants to protect us and empower us to be in control of our lives.

Parenting is a seriously tough job. Our parents aren't perfect. They can't be. They're human...just like us. But they do the best they can with the resources they have at the time.

Have you ever asked your parents what their childhood was like? It's kind of fun, and it helped me understand more about them and how they were disciplined by their parents.

God has your parents on their own faith journey to make them more like Him, just as He has you on yours. Your parents are responsible to work through the way their parents raised them and to align those experiences with what they learn from God's Word.

Of course, parents aren't all the same. Some are strict; others are more laid-back. And you may not have parents who know Jesus. Or you may have only a dad or only a mom in your home. That can be tough.

Take time to pray for your parents. If they don't know Jesus, set the example. Ask God to give you opportunities to share your faith with them. Perhaps He wants to use you to lead them to Jesus.

You will soon be out from under your parents' discipline. Maybe you already are. But God will always be faithful to lovingly discipline and train you, not in an abusive way, but because He deeply loves you and cares about you. Remember that the ultimate goal is to glorify God and become more like Jesus—and that's being totally God's!

What's a Girl to Do?

I don't know what your parental situation is, but I challenge you to honor the people who are responsible for you. Unless you have been asked to do something against God's will, try to respect those who are in authority over you at this time. Doing so is great training for following Christ as we grow.

Totally Talkin' with God

Father, I pray for all parents. I ask that You grant them wisdom in raising us girls who desire to be totally Yours. Our parents may not understand our desire if they do not know You, and if that is so, I pray for their salvation. Thank You for loving me enough to discipline me when I need the training. I want to be more like You. In Jesus' name, amen.

Authentic Fellowship

I thank my God every time I remember you.
PHILIPPIANS 1:3

Do you have dinner at home with your family at least a few nights a week? Do you go on vacations together? Family dates? Maybe group activities once a week with your friends?

The early church had the right idea about true and meaningful fellowship between believers. Christians sat together and listened to the teachings of the apostles. They studied hard and supported each other. They ate together and prayed together. They shared all their belongings with one another and with those in need. Every day they met with glad and sincere hearts, devoted to God. (See Acts 2:42-47.) Their Christian fellowship includes these characteristics:

> devotion to the teaching of God's Word
>
> hanging out and spending time together
>
> sharing a meal together
>
> praying together

If we look closely, this passage does not say that single people mingled only with other singles. Or teens with teens, children with children, married couples with married couples. The believers described in Acts were unified, regardless of their season in life. Their friendship was grounded in their common love for Jesus Christ.

We can learn a lot about life from our precious "senior saints." They can give us wisdom from their own life journeys. And we can even learn from the little toddler romping around joyfully and singing songs to Jesus. We are all the body of Christ—and His body is beautiful! All we have to do is take the time to listen and enjoy being together.

It's easy to gather around those with whom we have the most in common, like those who are our own age. And this is not a bad thing. We need friendships with others who are in the same season of life. However, we can miss out on so much if we forget to open our eyes and see others around us.

Do you have fellowship with believers who have walked with Christ longer than you have? Or do you have married friends who are inspirations to you? Have you ever thought about volunteering in the children's department of your local church?

If you answered no to any of the questions above, ask God to open your heart to new areas in which He may want to stretch you. You will be surprised at the blessings and wisdom you will receive! And you may even have fun! You won't regret stepping up and reaching out to the body of believers God has placed in your life for this season.

What's a Girl to Do?

Special friends come along only a few times in our lives. They may not look like what we expect, but they are always good for us and part of God's plan. Reach out of your comfort zone and meet new believers—young and old. You will be amazed!

Totally Talkin' with God

Father, thank You for the blessing of friendships on earth. Special sisters in Christ can bring much joy. I pray my friends and I may devote ourselves to Your teaching, fellowship together, eat together, and pray together, just as the believers did in Acts. Give me strength to reach out and fellowship with new people as well. In Jesus' name, amen.

Honoring Your Parents

Children, obey your parents in the Lord, for this is right.
EPHESIANS 6:1 NASB

Imagine Jesus as a toddler, learning to talk, walk, and giggle. What were His birthday parties like? It's hard for me to imagine that Jesus had parents and grew up like every other toddler and young kid today. But He was fully human—just like you and me. (And fully God too!)

Though we don't have much information about Jesus' life before His ministry began, we do know about one incident that occurred when He was 12 years old. He and His family traveled to Jerusalem for the feast of Passover. After a number of days had passed, Joseph and Mary headed home with a caravan of family and friends. They assumed Jesus was with them in the group somewhere.

A day passed before Joseph and Mary realized Jesus was not with them. They hurried back to Jerusalem and spent three whole days searching before finally finding Him. (See Luke 2:41-51.)

As expected, Mary was not pleased. She reacted the way most moms would and probably said something like "Jesus, why did You do this to us? Your dad and I have been worried sick! We've looked for You for three days!"

Jesus politely replied, "Why were you looking for Me? Didn't you know I'd be in My Father's house?" He was actually in the temple teaching the teachers! At 12 years of age! So cool.

Notice Jesus didn't yell. He didn't throw a fit or tell Joseph and Mary they were crazy. He wasn't disrespectful. He honored them. The Bible says He was obedient to them. That means Jesus didn't get frustrated and act out in disobedience when He and His parents had a misunderstanding. Instead, He honored them and continued to obey.

Here are some ways to help you become totally God's when it comes to respecting and honoring your parents:

- Try your best to keep a calm tone. Avoid raising your voice when addressing your parents. Whether in conflict or not, speak with respect and control.

- Trust is super hard to regain once it's lost. Do your best to be honest and up-front with your parents.
- This may sound odd, but ask your parents about their lives. Focus on hobbies they enjoy. Ask them about their job and other interests. You'll find they will be pleased and open up to you on a new level.

Whatever you do, be sincere. Don't just pretend to be nice to your parents so you can get what you want. That won't work anyway. Today, choose to honor and respect your parents. You won't regret it!

What's a Girl to Do?

In your journal, list some areas you feel weak in, especially areas that cause big fights with your parents or other authorities. Then pray over the list. Give it all to God and ask Him to help you change your behavior.

Totally Talkin' with God

Father, Jesus did come as a human. He had parents and siblings, just like me. You are our ultimate Father, but You have put me under the authority of others as well. Help me to be respectful. Help me to be obedient so long as I can also follow Your commands. In Jesus' name, amen.

A Hurting Generation

They will rebuild the ancient ruins and restore the
places long devastated; they will renew the ruined
cities that have been devastated for generations.

ISAIAH 61:4

During my senior year in high school, my class went on a hayride and sat around a bonfire together at a nearby camp. The crackling of the flickering fire at the center of the circle drew our attention.

My friends shared stories that night—stories that surprised most others in the group. Stories of heartache, pain, and deep hurt. The openness of one led to the vulnerability of another. Before I knew it, one by one, my friends began talking about who they were, what they were going through, and how they felt about the class, family, and friends.

Many said they were distant from God (and I went to a private Christian high school). Most didn't know how to reconnect with Him. Others had been deeply hurt by family members who were supposed to love them. Some had watched their parents split up.

Divorce affects girls in many ways but especially in their educational success and their adult romantic relationships. Also, girls in stepfamilies are more likely to struggle with anxiety and depression than girls from intact families. And girls tend to blame themselves for their parents' divorce.

During that night of sharing, nobody felt how freezing cold it was outside. We were all lost in the depth of one another's heartache. And although not everybody got a chance to share that night, those who did were glad they did.

We are a hurting generation that has been often misunderstood, abused, and unheard. We desire to have someone listen to us, hear the cry of our hearts, and continue to love us.

Youth is seen as a time of transition, recklessness, selfishness, and stress. For many teens, like a lot of my friends at the bonfire, youth is full of sad times. It can be a season that robs them of the life they dream of. Still, they walk around trying to fake a smile.

Healing a hurting generation takes a big act. An act only Jesus can do. His nail-scarred hands reach out and press gently on our bleeding hearts. Pain shoots through our bodies, but gradually the bleeding subsides and healing begins.

Our generation may be a little reckless, but we are also wounded. Now more than ever, I suggest we stick together. Build relationships with Christ and other Christian girls. Find mentors, role models, caring parents... anyone you can trust in the Lord and look up to. Ask them for advice and guidance. Share your difficult times with them. And walk the path of righteousness. Together with Christ, we can help each other heal!

What's a Girl to Do?

Our generation is lost in the world. But we are the remnant God has put on earth. We are the light that shines in the darkness. I challenge us to shine for Jesus. We can be the ones God uses to heal the brokenness in the lives of our friends and peers.

Totally Talkin' with God

Father, rebuild my life in You. Just as the wise man built his house upon the rock, so I want to build my life on Jesus—the Rock. Keep my feet from walking down reckless paths and my mind from making poor decisions. Help my light to shine bright so all will see it and praise Jesus. In His name, amen.

Unsaved Girlfriends

Do not be misled: "Bad company corrupts good character."
<small>1 CORINTHIANS 15:33</small>

Good friends—they're with us in the good times and the bad. They seem to love us unconditionally. And they "get us" on a level no one else can.

Sometimes, though, friends sway our decisions in the wrong direction. Their influence can outweigh that of our parents and even God. Our friends may be with us during hard times, but should they have the power to tell us what's right and wrong? True and false? Fun and boring? Sometimes I am torn. I think to myself, *They've got my back. I need to have theirs.*

In that case, is it okay to be friends with non-Christians? Sure. We all hang with those who either don't know Jesus or say they do but don't act like it. We need to be an influence to them.

But you should be aware of some things about your non-Christian friends. Even if we have the best of intentions and think we are not going to back down in our beliefs, the truth is, constantly hanging around nonbelievers weakens our drive to live for Christ. And temptations are everywhere: drinking, bad language, skimpy clothes, gossip, casual sex, drugs. But here are a few ways you can stand strong:

- Try to form close relationships with friends who will encourage you to live for Christ.
- If you have a particular issue with a certain temptation (like porn, drinking, swearing, or an eating disorder), choose to hang with Christians who don't struggle in the same area you do.
- Be careful to guard your heart.

Like I said before, non-Christian friends are okay to have. Just don't compromise your beliefs or identity in Christ just to impress a friend. By all means, reach out to people in the love of Jesus. Be ready to tell them why you follow Him. You never can tell—maybe God will use you to help a friend believe in Jesus. You could be a part of someone you care about coming to eternal salvation because you stood up for what you believed. Now *that* would be awesome!

What's a Girl to Do?

We should never ditch all our non-Christian friends. But we will have some tough decisions to make, especially if we have lots of close non-Christian friends. Pray and ask God to give you the strength to tell them about Jesus and to bring you some friends who are following Him.

Totally Talkin' with God

Father, the thought of dumping all my nonbelieving friends sounds so mean. Christ wouldn't do that, would He? Lord, help me to make the right decisions about my friends. Give me the strength to stand strong in Jesus. I love You, and I want my friends to know You. In Jesus' name, amen.

It Can Be Lonely Being Alone

When all things are subjected to Him, then the Son
Himself also will be subjected to the One who subjected
all things to Him, so that God may be all in all.
1 CORINTHIANS 15:28 NASB

Being alone is not always fun. I try to act like it's not a big deal, but when I am alone, I usually find myself texting my friends or getting on Facebook. I don't like being alone because it feels...well, lonely!

Loneliness isn't just for those without boyfriends. Even the most popular girls can be lonely. We can be in a roomful of people and still feel lonely. Our list of friends can have hundreds of names, and we can still feel lonely. We can get text after text from friends who want to talk to us and still feel lonely.

When we're lonely, we often feel as if no one cares. Nothing fits. Nothing seems to satisfy. Nothing we attempt works. Maybe we have lost a friend or family member. In that case, loneliness feels like something is missing. When we feel lonely, all we want to do is end the pain, so we look for fulfillment somewhere.

Jesus has already claimed us as His own. He stakes out His property and takes up residence in us. Oftentimes, though, He finds Himself pushed around by things trying to move in on His territory—things like friends, popularity, boys, clothes, beauty, money, academic achievement, and athletics.

Then one day we listen to Jesus. We decide to give Him first place in our lives and in our hearts. And you know what? We begin to experience true joy and a fulfilled life! The truth is, Jesus is the only one who will fill our emptiness. Regardless of how hard we try to stuff our hearts with other things, they will never do the trick. We will become lonelier and lonelier.

If you are tired of feeling lonely and searching for something more, ask God today what it means to trust Him with your life—even the painful parts. Then give it to Him. You will be glad you did!

What's a Girl to Do?

Loneliness can be a difficult thing. And sometimes even Jesus doesn't seem to fill our lonely hearts. Stop today and imagine Him saying to you, *I can fill you. Come to Me.*

Totally Talkin' with God

Father, my heart will be satisfied only with You. Jesus is my best friend. Remind me of that daily, Lord. I ask You to help me take out the stuff I use to fill my heart and leave more room for Jesus, who knows what I really need. In His name, amen.

No *I* in *Team*

*Do you not know that in a race all the runners run, but only
one gets the prize? Run in such a way as to get the prize.*

1 CORINTHIANS 9:24

"Runners on your mark...set..." *Bang!* If you've competed in a track meet, those words can put butterflies in your belly.

Track meets cannot be won without the efforts of the entire team. A track meet is won when many individual members of the team perform well and contribute to the team score. As coaches often remind their teams, there is no *I* in *team*.

If you have trained for an athletic event, you understand the amount of discipline required. "Everyone who competes in the games goes into strict training" (1 Corinthians 9:25).

Ever notice that those who walk during the marathon don't win the race? As a Christian, I want to run, not walk. Walkers don't win running races. When I keep only a walker's pace in my growth as a Christian, I might as well tell God, *Hey, I just don't want to put much effort into this relationship thing, Lord. Sorry.*

By the way, the Bible is not literally saying we all have to go buy running shoes. Actually, God knows that physical training has some value, but spiritual training has value for all things (1 Timothy 4:8). *Running for Christ* describes a mind-set or attitude about our relationship with Him. It includes being willing to exert some effort, practice, and develop.

Through our belief in Jesus, we are already in the race. The question is, do we simply want to finish, or do we want to finish well? For me, I want to finish well. The training part sounds painful and not much fun, but I will do it for Jesus.

After the starter shouts out those few special words and fires the gun, runners with all body shapes, sizes, and talent set off to...to what, lose? No—to win! I don't know any athlete who races just to give up, to come in last, to hang up the towel. And the same is true in our race for Christ. We should train for that by reading the Bible, praying, spending time around other Christians, and serving the Lord. And as we train, lo and behold, we're already picking up speed. And hey—we're doin' pretty good!

Athletes know that winning the prize is worth the effort of training— even winning just a temporary medal or award. Our prize is so much better! God will say to each one of us, "Well done, good and faithful servant."

What's a Girl to Do?

You may love a challenge. You may enjoy the training and hard work that goes into reaching a goal. Well, our goal as Christians is to live for Christ. Let's run, not walk, for the one who loves us!

Totally Talkin' with God

Father, You have done so much for me. The least I can do is put some effort into my relationship with You. The thing is, I can so easily put hard work into the things of this world, but for You, I just don't. I'm so sorry. Forgive me. And help me to do better. I love You, Lord. In Jesus' name, amen.

7

CHOICES, DECISIONS, CONSEQUENCES

*Devotions on the power of choice and
deciding to live for Christ*

Soul-Poisoning

Forget about deciding what's right for each other. Here's what
you need to be concerned about: that you don't get in the way
of someone else, making life more difficult than it already is.
ROMANS 14:13 MSG

One of the greatest debates I have heard among Christians is whether or not it is acceptable to drink alcohol, smoke, chew, and date boys who do. Ha ha—I'm slightly kidding, but the truth is, there are a number of things we Christians don't have a lot of answers to. From drinking alcohol to dating relationships to what we're allowed to eat, the Bible doesn't necessarily just come right out and tell us.

Still, many Christians today are quick to make judgments about somebody's character and spiritual growth based on behaviors that tend to be questionable—*to them*. In Romans, Paul addresses this dilemma.

> None of us are permitted to insist on our own way in these matters. It's God we are answerable to...not each other... Forget about deciding what's right for each other. Here's what you need to be concerned about: that you don't get in the way of someone else, making life more difficult than it already is...
>
> If you confuse others by making a big issue over what they eat or don't eat, you're no longer a companion with them in love, are you? These, remember, are persons for whom Christ died. Would you risk sending them to hell over an item in their diet? Don't you dare let a piece of God-blessed food become an occasion of soul-poisoning! (Romans 14:7-8,13,15-16).

We must also be careful that our own self-criticism doesn't cause others to stumble as well. Here's an example: You and Julie are friends. Julie is a new believer, and she looks to you for answers to questions about being a Christian. God has given you many opportunities to speak the truth into Julie's life. One day, Julie confides in you that she is anorexic and struggling with her weight. You explain to her that her body is God's home and she is made in His image. You express your desire to help her through this difficult time.

The next day, you and Julie go to lunch. After you get your food and sit at the table, you say, "I hate my body. I so need to lose some weight before homecoming." And you proceed to shove your tray of food to the side, sipping a soda instead.

See the problem? You told Julie she needs help, but now you keep yourself from eating in front of her, reinforcing the message she already struggles with: *I'm fat. Nobody will like me unless I lose weight.* Can she really listen to your advice or look up to you as a stronger believer now?

I'm not perfect. I struggle with judging myself and other people too. We all do. But I desire with all my heart to do as God says and make life easier for others, not more difficult. I hope you do too. Whether it's seeing somebody behaving a certain way you don't agree with or behaving in a way that will cause somebody else to stumble, be careful of not being quick to "soul poison" anybody. If we can accomplish this, even on small scale, we will be making a real difference in people's lives and be that much closer to becoming girls who are totally God's.

What's a Girl to Do?

Let's try to keep from judging others—not just this week, but for good. Ask God to convict you when you begin to say something you shouldn't.

Totally Talkin' with God

Father, it is so easy to say something mean or judgmental. Everyone does it. Help me to be a good witness to those around me. I desire to open my mouth in love and purity. I love you, Lord. In Jesus' name, amen.

Be Careful, Little Eyes

We don't have a priest who is out of touch with our reality. He's
been through weakness and testing, experienced it all—all
but the sin. So let's walk right up to him and get what he
is so ready to give. Take the mercy, accept the help.
HEBREWS 4:15 MSG

Picture this: You and several friends decide to hang at Rob's house. Popcorn and a movie. Everyone hurries to find a decent seat in Rob's living room. You told your parents of the movie night at Rob's, and they did what they always do—they called Rob's parents to find out what the movie was. They thought the film was okay, so you were good to go.

Into the living room walks Rob. "Hey, my parents are asleep. Let's watch a different movie—one with a little more 'action,' if you know what I mean."

Then the movie comes on. "A little more action" doesn't come close to describing this film. You want to close your eyes at all the violence, evil, and nudity, but you are too embarrassed. Now the images are burned in your brain, and you're afraid to walk the two blocks home alone in the dark.

Ugh...what should you do?

Ever felt that way? Leaving Rob's house would have been like committing social suicide, but that probably would have been the best move.

Protecting our eyes and ears is a constant battle. We are bombarded with images of blood, violence, and nudity in the movies and on TV. And unfortunately, vulgar language, sexual harassment, and physical abuse are sad realities in many of our lives. What do we do? We can't walk around with paper bags over our heads and earplugs stuck in our ears. That would be pretty dangerous, and we'd look a bit strange!

It comes down to making better choices. If something will cause us to hear or see something we shouldn't, we can always change course and veer another direction. Jesus tells us that He always leaves a door open for escape when we're in over our heads (1 Corinthians 10:13).

The images or voices you've seen and heard will come back when you least expect them. Before you know it, you will find yourself unaffected and tempted to go along with things you really don't believe in.

This is not the goal. As girls who are totally God's, we need to ask Jesus to help us stay strong in the middle of hard situations. He's been through it all and understands our weaknesses, as our focus verse reminds us.

Sure, it would be easier to live in a bubble and never be around sin. But that's impossible while on earth. Remember, we can do all things through Christ who gives us strength (Philippians 4:13). We can walk out on movies, ask others to tone down the language, and live purely in a sinful world. God promises to give you the strength.

Take care of your eyes. Be bold and faithfully stand firm today and always!

What's a Girl to Do?

Let's make a specific effort to stand out for Christ. Let's pray and ask God to help us be bold and do what's right.

Totally Talkin' with God

Father, this world is full of temptations, full of things that fill my mind with unrighteousness. I know I don't always avoid these situations. Sometimes I can even run toward them. I want to change. Help me to not become like the bad things I see and hear. Guard my mind and spirit and give me the strength to choose to do what is right. I love you, Jesus! In Your name, amen.

You've Got Talent...Now What?

Well done, good and faithful servant! You have been
faithful with a few things; I will put you in charge of many
things. Come and share your master's happiness!
MATTHEW 25:21

Talented people come in all shapes, sizes, and ages. When they put their talent to work, they are so good at what they do, they beat all the competition and make a name for themselves.

But what about people who have talent but don't care? They come in all shapes and sizes too. They are still good at what they do, but they are either too scared or too lazy to practice and become the best. Many of us have seen their ability and know they would go far—if they only tried.

Jesus told a lot of stories when He walked the earth. One was about talents. A talent in Jesus' day was a unit of weight (one talent was about seventy-five pounds). People measured money by weighing it, so in this case, a talent is a pile of gold or some other precious stone or metal. As Jesus' parable became famous, people began to refer to special abilities as talents.

The parable of the talents is about a man who entrusts some of his property to his servants. One servant received five talents, another received two talents, and another received one. The servant with five talents immediately invested his five talents and gained five more. The servant with two talents did the same and gained two more talents. But the servant with one talent dug a hole in the ground and buried his master's money.

When the master returned, he said something like this: "Okay, so what did you do with what I gave you?" The master was pleased with the investment and return of the first two servants. But the servant who buried his talent did not get such a happy response. The master was so upset with his final servant that he took the talent back.

Which servant reminds you most of yourself? Are you like the first servant, who has lots of talent and uses it wisely for God? Are you like the second servant, who has a little talent but uses it for God? Or are you like the third servant, who didn't invest his talent for God at all?

If the third servant had done as his master requested, he probably would have received the same happy response. He would have been told, "Well done; I am pleased with you."

Here's the bottom line: Whatever your "talent" situation may be, don't be like the third servant and bury your gifts until our Master's return. Instead, use what God has entrusted to you for His glory. One of the best gifts He has given us is the gift of eternal life through His Son Jesus (Romans 6:23). Begin with that. You have the gift of salvation! Share it. Tell others. What else has He given you? Invest your gift, and God will bring the increase!

What's a Girl to Do?

Pray and ask the Lord what gifts you have and how you can use them for Him. Then wait on Him—He'll let you know. Remember, no one but God may notice what you do. Don't worry about whether others see. God is the only one who matters!

Totally Talkin' with God

Father, You are a wonderful Master who gives good gifts. I want to use the talents You have entrusted to me exactly the way You have intended. Please guide me. I really want to do Your will with what You have given me. I love You! In Jesus' name, amen.

Power Struggle

I do not understand what I do. For what I want
to do I do not do, but what I hate I do.
ROMANS 7:15

Remember watching old cartoons and seeing a character who had a moral dilemma? An angel and a demon appear on his shoulders. As the cartoon character thinks about what decision to make, the demon whispers his tempting enticements: "Go ahead, no one will notice...C'mon, this will be fun...Don't be such a chicken..."

The angel defends what is good and says, "Careful, you may regret this later...Someone will get hurt...Don't follow the crowd...Do the right thing..."

Sounds kind of like real life, huh? These voices represent our conscience. But I think the spiritual battle raging around us is bigger than we realize. I believe those old cartoons were closer to the truth than we know.

When we face a moral dilemma, we often have thoughts about what may feel good, what may seem fun, what consequences may occur, and the risks of getting caught. We all have weak areas bent toward sin, and the enemy knows this.

The apostle Paul was acutely aware of his weakness. In today's verses, Paul explains how he continually struggles with the pull of sin in his life. Sin can lead even some of the strongest Christians to make poor decisions. Yet Paul had hope.

> If I know the law but still can't keep it, and if the power of sin within me keeps sabotaging my best intentions, I need help! I realize I don't have what it takes. I decide to do good, but I don't really do it...I truly delight in God's commands, but it's pretty obvious that not all of me joins in that delight...The answer, thank God, is that Jesus Christ can and does" (Romans 7:20-25 MSG).

Wow! Paul basically says that we are helpless to defeat sin without Christ. We're in an invisible spiritual battle. If we are in Christ, we have the Spirit of God and have been released or freed from the power of sin. God offered His own sinless life as a sacrifice for you and me. He defeated the sin that entangles us every day. Praise the Lord!

Lean on the power of the Holy Spirit. Listen to His still, small voice telling you the right way to go. Ask for God's wisdom and claim the victory over sin in your life today!

What's a Girl to Do?

We all make mistakes. We fall into sin, and Satan pushes us down, hoping we will forget that we have freedom through Christ. We need to set our minds on the things of the Spirit. If you're not sure what those are, read the Bible. Romans 8:5 is a good place to start.

Totally Talkin' with God

Father, I do not want to sin. I know that I'm young in my faith and that as I choose to grow in You, Your Spirit will help me to become strong. I long for that, Lord. Help me to begin to follow the leading of Your Spirit so I can win the battle over sin. In Jesus' name, amen.

What Is Success?

I denied myself nothing my eyes desired; I refused my heart no
pleasure. My heart took delight in all my work, and this was the
reward for all my labor. Yet when I surveyed all that my hands had
done and what I had toiled to achieve, everything was meaningless,
a chasing after the wind; nothing was gained under the sun.
ECCLESIASTES 2:10-11

I recently heard an incredible definition for the word *tragedy*: "succeeding in the things of life that don't matter." It made me think about the things I spend time on, get obsessed with, and cry over that really don't matter.

Our culture seems to be obsessed with success. It defines success by the amount of money we have, how well we're known, or how many friends we have. We may be successful if we've achieved recognition for something we did, like receiving an award at school, winning a sports championship, or being elected class president. Such achievements are wonderful and should be noted. But at the end of the day, I'm telling you now, the trophies will collect dust. Lots of dust!

I struggle with this as much as anyone. Many times, I don't give God the glory He deserves. I totally forget or neglect to acknowledge who really did the work. Here's what should go through my head: First, God made me. I wouldn't be here without Him. Second, He gives me the talents I have and opportunities to use them. Third, successes that come from those opportunities are all gifts from Him (James 1:17).

I'm not taking anything away from your own efforts. You have to work hard to accomplish great things. God calls us to work hard, to run the race, to strive for the best. But it should all be for His glory! Don't strive to measure up to the world's standards. Paul wrote that we should "fix our eyes not on what is seen but on what is unseen, for what is seen is temporary and what is unseen is eternal" (2 Corinthians 4:18). The things in this life are fleeting. She who dies with the most toys, still dies. Are you fixing your eyes on the unseen? Or are you chasing after success as the world defines it?

Ask God today to show you what true success is. Remember, success should reveal eternal significance. Live with that goal in mind. And remember to give Him the glory!

What's a Girl to Do?

Are you succeeding in life at things that don't matter?

Totally Talkin' with God

Father, I love to call You Father. You are my true Daddy—Abba. I love You. Please help me to not be afraid to look different from people who are enamored with this world. Give me the heart to follow You, Lord, regardless of where You may lead me. Show me the true meaning of success and to focus on that. In Jesus' name, amen.

Every Thought

We are destroying speculations and every lofty thing
raised up against the knowledge of God, and we are taking
every thought captive to the obedience of Christ.
2 CORINTHIANS 10:5 NASB

I love the book *Confessions of a Shopaholic*! And when the movie came out recently, my mom and I were among the first in line at our local theater to see it. We had a great time laughing until we hurt and elbowing each other when we could relate to what was happening on-screen. My belly and side ached for days!

The movie depicts a life lived on impulse. Becky Bloomwood is the main character, who struggles to control her desire to shop. Becky views shopping as a stress reliever and gives in to her internal impulses to buy whatever she believes she needs—until she receives her credit card bill. Wow! Once she is faced with reality and enormous debt, she begins to understand the importance of thinking before acting!

Oswald Chambers, who wrote the devotional *My Utmost for His Highest,* said this about 2 Corinthians 10:5: "So much Christian work today has never been disciplined, but has simply come into being by impulse... But true determination and zeal are found in obeying God, not in the inclination to serve Him that arises from our own undisciplined human nature."

Mr. Chambers is criticizing the "do it now" mentality. He says we need to take our thoughts captive, make them prisoners for Jesus, and do what He wants for our lives.

Have you ever noticed that many mature Christians take time and think before they act? They pray and search God's heart on issues before making decisions. Mr. Chambers tells us that these Christians are disciplining their thoughts and actions. They don't quickly do what they want, but consider first what God wants and choose to do His will.

God says not to be impulsive. If the apostle James used today's vernacular, he might have said, "Listen. Don't be thinking you know the future—'cuz you don't. Only God does. And it's His will that will be done. So you better talk to Him before you announce any plans." (See James 4:12-15.)

God desires that you rely on His will. Align your life, thoughts, dreams, desires, and passions with His. When you do, you won't be disappointed! And you may even be able to keep your green scarf. (You've just got to read the book!)

What's a Girl to Do?

I'm convicted that our world is all about instant gratification. Do it now or else. God wants us to wait on Him and His will (Psalm 27:14). No more jumping the gun. Instead, let's ask for God's help today in waiting on His will in our lives.

Totally Talkin' with God

Father, sometimes out of good intentions I do things quickly and then regret my rash decisions. But You even use that to teach me a valuable lesson: I need to wait on You and seek Your will, not mine. Show me Your will, Lord, today and always. In Jesus' name, amen.

Bananas, Strawberries, and Self-Control

*The fruit of the Spirit is love, joy, peace, patience,
kindness, goodness, faithfulness, gentleness, and self-
control. Against such things there is no law.*

GALATIANS 5:22-23

Do you like the title of today's devotional? When I hear the word *fruit*, I instantly picture ripe red strawberries, curvy yellow bananas, juicy green apples, and fuzzy peaches. The last thing that comes to my mind is the fruit of the Spirit. But the fruit of the Spirit is the behavioral goal list for Christians.

I'm lucky if I show a few of these character traits, let alone all of them! Seeing this fruit grow in our lives seems too much to hope for. How can we do it? The Bible tells us that by living by God's Spirit, we won't be so tempted to sin (Galatians 5:16). When we're led by the Spirit, we'll naturally do good things in the name of Christ. If we are living by the Spirit, we may reach out to a hurting classmate or even someone we don't know very well. But we do it all through the love of Jesus working through us—not in our own strength.

Reading the Old Testament, you'll get an idea of all the rules the Israelites had to follow. But did you know that God gave them the Law so they would realize they *can't* do it alone? So their own sin would get in the way of ever being able to obey the Law? God wanted them and us to see that following the Law or being saved and producing fruit are impossible because of our sin. We can't do it! We always mess up. This helps us understand how awesome Jesus' sacrifice really was!

The fruit of the Spirit has to grow in us. This growth occurs through an ongoing, close relationship with God through Jesus. The more we deny doing only what we want to do, the more we will begin to notice the sprouting of this wonderful fruit in our lives.

What's a Girl to Do?

We can do nothing apart from God. He is the one who gives us faith to believe and be saved, and He is the one who helps us turn away from our sinful nature. So the best way to begin growing fruit is to pray through each item in Galatians 5:22-23 and ask God to grow each one in you. Then watch for opportunities and listen for His guidance in your life.

Totally Talkin' with God

Father, thank You for the gift of the Holy Spirit, who guides me in love to bear fruit that lasts. Enable me through Your Spirit to deny my desire to sin and to live Your way. I love You, Lord. In Jesus' name, amen.

Have You Done Something Really Bad?

If we confess our sins, He is faithful and righteous to forgive
us our sins and to cleanse us from all unrighteousness.
1 JOHN 1:9 NASB

When I was a little girl, I woke up one morning and decided that for one day, I would be perfect. I wouldn't get sassy with my mom. I wouldn't get annoyed by my little brother's whining. Somehow, I thought that if I just tried hard enough, I could be good.

But let's face it—we all mess up sometimes. Maybe we pass notes in class, cheat on a test, or spread rumors about a girl we don't like. Maybe, though, you have done something way bigger, something you haven't ever told anybody about.

Lies, disrespect, anger, gossip, pride, sexual behavior—whatever you may be hiding, God's Word has something to say about it:

> The heart is hopelessly dark and deceitful
> a puzzle that no one can figure out.
> But I, GOD, search the heart
> and examine the mind.
> I get to the root of things.
> I treat them as they really are,
> not as they pretend to be (Jeremiah 17:9-10 MSG).

God knows your heart. Are you trying to hide the sin in your life? Don't. Jesus knows every single thing about you and me—even the stuff we think we can hide.

Does that scare you? It doesn't have to. The God of the entire universe doesn't just search our hearts; He actually *did* something about them. Jesus' death on the cross wasn't about warm fuzzies. It was about love— the greatest kind of love you and I could ever experience. A love that took God's punishment for all of the sins we've ever committed or ever will.

Jesus' love for us is so amazing. We can no more *earn* His love than we can make the sun shine. God loves us for who we are as His daughters, and we can do nothing to change that.

But Megan, you might be thinking, *you don't know me. I've done too much. I'm too bad for God to forgive.* But that is exactly why Jesus Christ came. The more messed up our lives are, the more we need God's grace.

And that grace is a gift. It's free—not something we can earn. Regardless of what you've done, Jesus took God's wrath for you. The Bible says that God is ready and waiting not only to forgive us but also to clean up all the nasty, rotten trash in our hearts. God promises to cleanse you from *all* unrighteousness.

No sin is so big that God's forgiveness isn't greater still. So don't try to hide from God. Tell Him all about what you've done. He can't wait to say, *I love you...and I forgive you.*

What's a Girl to Do?

No sin is too big for God. Remember that. Regardless of what the world says, God wants to forgive our sins. If you've got Jesus, you are already forgiven. But if you don't, choose now to believe in Him! Go to "Do You Really Know?" (page 13) and accept Jesus as Lord and Savior. Receive forgiveness today.

Totally Talkin' with God

Father, thank You for forgiving me of my mistakes. I make them every day, so I'm eternally grateful that Jesus has made a way for me to be reconciled to You. I pray for those who do not know Him. I pray that they won't wait to believe, but that they too may be forgiven. I love you, Lord. You are the best. In Jesus' name, amen.

8
CUTIES, SEX, AND SEXY

Devotions on guys, dating, and all that stuff

Reading Him like a Book

Above all else, guard your heart, for it is the wellspring of life.
PROVERBS 4:23

Picture this. A new boy just moved in three houses down the street from where you live. You watched him help his dad around the house for about two weeks before the school year started. You know he is cute and looks about your age. When the first day of school arrives, he is sitting only two seats away from you in homeroom, and all of the girls are talking about him.

During the first week of school, he somehow finds out you live in the same neighborhood. By Friday he asks you to help him get used to his new surroundings. Yes! He noticed!

So on a warm Saturday morning you go for a walk around your neighborhood. You are really hitting it off. You find out he played in a Christian band where he used to live. His dad is a pastor. He seems genuine, sweet, nice, caring.

From then on you read something into every move he makes. You become more and more excited because you see sure signs he likes you. And all the while you totally discount any signs that he's just enjoying a simple friendship.

Our minds take our hearts to places they should not go. And we become confused.

In a state of anxiety you think that if you don't snatch him up now, the rapture may beat you to it. Or worse, another girl. You check his Facebook page every opportunity you have. Did somebody post something? You must act now!

I have often heard people say that life is 10 percent what happens to us and 90 percent how we react to it. Our attitudes make all the difference today, and they will determine our success in the future.

I know it's tough if all of your friends have boyfriends and you don't. You can get lonely and feel like the third wheel. Or the fifth wheel, tagging along in groups of couples. You're alone, not being chased, and left wondering, *What's wrong with me?*

But to be honest, what's wrong with being single? Why not be grateful for the place where God has you right now? Why read something into every little thing a guy does just to be noticed? Enjoy your singleness. Get to know God first. Read His Word. I've heard people say that you should be so close with God that a guy must pursue Him to get to you. Now *that* is guarding your heart!

What's a Girl to Do?

Don't let boys rule your world. Remember, you should be so close to God that a guy has to valiantly pursue Him to get to you! Pray today that God will give you the strength to know that He is all you need!

Totally Talkin' with God

Father, my heart is so fragile. I just want to be loved. Remind me that I already am. You love me. I have friends and family who love me. And I love You, Lord. In Jesus' name, amen.

Guys

Finally, brethren, whatever is true, whatever is honorable,
whatever is right, whatever is pure, whatever is lovely,
whatever is of good repute, if there is any excellence and
if anything worthy of praise, dwell on these things.
PHILIPPIANS 4:8 NASB

When guys began to pay attention to me and the possibility of dating was close, life became quite interesting in the Clinton household. Let's just say I started to see more of my dad's extensive gun collection he primarily uses for hunting purposes.

I bet you're wondering why I chose this verse for a devotional on guys. After all, we need to stay as far away from boys as we can until we are married, right?

Just kidding! The truth is, guys *can* be great friends, and eventually, in time, one may even become your husband and partner for life. But I have seen so many girls get caught up in the drama of *needing* a boyfriend. They believe the world will end if they don't have someone to date. Life will not go on! They will never find true love! They fall into a pit of despair when their girlfriends get the guys and they remain without a relationship.

That is, until the magic day when *he* walks through the door. Tall, wavy hair, star of the basketball team, new in town—and he's available!

This is my chance, she tells herself. And soon, she's going on a date.

The relationship moves fast. It's fresh, exciting, new. And then it happens. Out of the blue, he moves on to an upperclassman. She finds herself single, and the drama begins again.

I included a list of girls' attitudes toward boys in my book *Totally God's*:

- Anxious Annie: "I've just got to have him."
- Hungry-for-Attention Hannah: "Since he talked to me, he must be totally into me."
- Mrs. Mary: "If I'm not married by 21, there is something wrong with me."

- Physical Phyllis: "If I give in to what he wants physically, I'm sure he'll love me forever."

- Friendly Faith: "We have been friends for so long now. I'm sure God wants us to be together."

- Prayerful Pattie: "God told me that boy was the one I would marry."

- Savior Sue: "He isn't a Christian, but I just know that if I date him he will get saved."

Which of these descriptions sounds most like you? Which girl do you readily identify with? Whether you date or not, frequent "head checks" and "heart checks" are highly recommended and needed in order to keep from falling into the desperately dating trap!

- Head check: Are you allowing this relationship to compromise any promises you have made to God and yourself?

- Heart check: Do you still remember that you have a desire within you to be loved, wanted, and safe? Are you dwelling on the truth that only God can provide this for you?

Let's stop the cycle of being desperate and in a hurry! It's time to let the guys be the pursuers, not the other way around. God intended for you to be sought after like a priceless treasure. And when it occurs just as God planned, it's truly amazing!

If you identified with one of the girls above, chances are you may have forgotten your first love—Jesus. Allow Him to fulfill your desires for romance, friendship, and love.

When a guy realizes you are sold out to God, he will have to find Him in order to find you. And *that's* being totally God's.

What's a Girl to Do?

As I suggested above, do a head and heart check on your guy situation. If you come out on the desperate side, don't fear. Now you know. Ask God to help you make wise relationship decisions. Learn to be contented without a guy and rely on God for love. The right one will come along in time.

Totally Talkin' with God

Father, I love You, and I know You love me more than any other person on earth can or will. Forgive me when I forget and I search for true love in the wrong places. Reassure my heart of Your unending and unconditional love, and give me the strength to do what You tell me, regardless of what others may say. In Jesus' name, amen.

How Far Is Too Far?

It is God's will that you should be sanctified: that you should
avoid sexual immorality; that each of you should learn to control
his [her] own body in a way that is holy and honorable.

1 THESSALONIANS 4:3-4

Oh, Tyler and I don't do much, just..." Ever heard that from a friend? Or, how about this: "It's not like we had *sex* or anything!"

So really, how far is too far? God created us with these feelings, right? He gave us these desires, and He talks about the importance of loving one another all throughout His Word, so why shouldn't we be able to express this love with our boyfriends?

To find a solid answer to these questions, first look at what Song of Solomon says about the importance of living a life of purity: "Don't excite love, don't stir it up, until the time is ripe—and you're ready" (Song of Solomon 8:4 MSG).

We all have the desire to be loved and feel accepted. Knowing that someone cares for us and wants to be with us—now *that's* exciting! Yet Solomon warns us to be careful. He understood where that desire can take us. Later in this same passage, he describes the powerful nature of love: "Many waters cannot quench love" (Song of Solomon 8:7).

What does this mean? It means we're human. And once we taste what love is like, it's difficult to stay physically pure. But it's important that we do.

So how far is too far? I'm sure you've heard of the term *technical virgin*. It means that as long as someone doesn't have sex, she's still a virgin. But virginity is about more than just physical affection. It's about guarding your heart (Proverbs 4:23) and keeping your life pure in every area.

In my book *Totally God's*, I wrote this:

> Your body is a gift—a beautiful gift—and on it is a name tag with
> the name of one man. If you let other guys touch your body and
> be rough with it, they will damage it and damage you. On your

wedding night, do you want to present your husband with a gift half opened, or worse, torn open and already used?

Perhaps you have already gone too far. I've talked to so many girls who have gone too far and feel devastated, ashamed, guilty, and unworthy of the love God originally planned for them. Some even continue to have sex and say to themselves, "I'm not a virgin anymore, so what's the use?"

But there's a distinct difference between being pure and being a virgin. It's important to understand that virginity can be lost, but your purity can be redeemed! Purity is found in the way we talk, what clothes we wear, the way we act, and most importantly, the state of our hearts. Paul tells Timothy to "flee the evil desires of youth, to pursue righteousness, faith, love and peace, along with those who call on the Lord out of a pure heart" (2 Timothy 2:22). Here's how you can pursue righteousness:

- Write down boundaries you need to establish for yourself both physically and emotionally.
- Study verses on living a pure life and think about how they apply to you.
- Pray and confess any sin you may have hidden and accept God's forgiveness.

Make a commitment to yourself (and your future husband) to live a life of purity, not only in the sexual sense but in every area of your life. You won't regret it!

What's a Girl to Do?

We can do all things through Christ who gives us strength (Philippians 4:13). Starting now, make a promise to God and to yourself to remain pure at all costs for His glory!

Totally Talkin' with God

Father, I stand on the promise of the Word that through Jesus, You are faithful to forgive me of all my sins. Lord, I want to remain pure, but I can't without Your help. All my hope is in You. In Jesus' name, amen.

The Lies We Believe

You will know the truth, and the truth will set you free.
JOHN 8:32

Have you ever been lied to? How did it make you feel? Betrayed, angry, frustrated, confused? I know the feeling—it really hurts!

Staring us in the face from about every magazine on the shelf are the how-tos of life:

"Four Easy Steps to Super-Sexy Hair"

"Getting the Perfect Date"

"Everything You Need to Be Prom Queen"

...and the list goes on and on.

Are these promises true? Of course not! Lies surround us every day. We are being lied to through television, magazines, books, music, and so much more. Deception is the enemy's sharpest tool. I think it's time we start fighting back and believing the truth!

In my discussions with girls of all ages, two major areas of deception come up every time: lies about self-identity and lies about sin.

Here's a lie about self-identity: "Physical beauty matters more than inner beauty."

If I could scream from the top of my lungs for all to hear, I would say, "You are beautiful!" Period. You are created by God—from nothing into something wonderful, beautiful, priceless! The truth is found in Proverbs 31:30: "Charm is deceptive, and beauty is fleeting; but a woman who fears the LORD is to be praised."

Yes, you will have bad hair days and times when you feel less than perfect. You will sometimes wish you could call "Do over!" and start again. It's okay. God isn't done with you yet! No, "He who began a good work in you will carry it on to completion" (Philippians 1:6).

Now, here's a lie about sin: "I can sin and get away with it because my sin isn't really that bad."

What is sin? Sin is any act that goes against God and His Word and breaks our relationship with Him. (See James 1:14-15.) It is an act based on a lie. We are told to believe, "Everybody is doing it... Go ahead, if it feels good to you... It's your body, and you can do whatever you want with it." When we act on these lies, we fall into bondage and are no longer living in God's freedom.

In the Ten Commandments, God lists some sins that He detests. They include sexual immorality, dishonoring your parents, lying, murder, and placing other gods before Him. Our world would say they're no big deal. But to a holy God, they are a huge deal!

We are all born in sin and deserve death. But God in His grace has given us a chance at something greater: the gift of salvation and eternal life through Jesus Christ's death on the cross. John 3:16 says, "God so loved the world that he gave his one and only Son, that whoever believes in him shall not perish but have eternal life." What a gift!

Satan is a liar and the father of all lies (John 8:44). If we desire to be totally God's, we will open our eyes to see the truth—God's truth. Choose today to stop believing the lies of the enemy. Live in the freedom of Christ!

What's a Girl to Do?

All we believe and do should be for the glory of God. We must begin to think before we act, basing every decision on truth—God's truth!

Totally Talkin' with God

Father, help me to recognize lies that are set before me every day. I want to live in freedom and the boundaries set for my life according to Your truth. I love You! In Jesus' name, amen.

Modesty? What's That?

Make up your mind not to put any stumbling
block or obstacle in your brother's way.
ROMANS 14:13

When girls wear revealing and provocative clothing, guys can start feeling crazy—and not in the funny sense of the word either. Guys are very visual and full of imagination. In today's verse, the apostle Paul warns us about becoming obstacles or stumbling blocks to our brothers in Christ.

I'm sure you've noticed fashion trends are all about tight-fitting, low-cut outfits. We see them on girls everywhere. School, the mall, parties—even in church! I'm not trying to sound strict and ultraconservative, but oh my!

When we put on that super cute outfit that screams, "Look at me," we not only cause guys to stumble but also stir up relational issues with girls. Our decisions about what we wear can lead to a few different scenarios:

- We could promote jealousy and envy in other girls. Both are wrong and can destroy our relationships.

- We could entice guys to think more about our bodies than our hearts or our minds, causing them to stumble.

Are we to blame when people fall into sin? No, they make their own choices. But if we entice them when we could do something to keep them from falling, we are selfish and irresponsible.

Suppose someone puts a smoldering cigarette in a trash can that happens to have some dry paper in it. A fire starts and consumes the area. Regardless of whether he is directly to blame, he is partly responsible. After all, he did choose not to put out the smoldering cigarette.

The same holds true for what we choose to wear. We need to own our choices instead of claiming, "It's the trend" or "I didn't know I looked that way."

Sure, modesty may not be popular. And we aren't completely to blame when other people sin. But I hate to think that what I may wear or what another girl may wear could cause my little brother, Zach, to struggle and become obsessed with women and sex. That's enough reason for me to be a little choosier about what I wear and how I wear it.

Use your body for God's glory, and don't be a stumbling block. Be someone who helps others stand for Christ and not fall for sin!

What's a Girl to Do?

Ask God to show you if you have outfits that are too revealing. Also ask God to convict you if you try to get attention from boys through what you wear or how you wear it. This exercise may make you a little uncomfortable, but God calls you to be to pure (1 Thessalonians 4:7), and He will help you do it!

Totally Talkin' with God

Father, thank You for helping me see that I can be a stumbling block for others when I choose to wear certain clothes. Help me to set personal boundaries and become aware of when I am causing others to stumble. In Jesus' name, amen.

True Love

This is love: not that we loved God, but that he loved
us and sent his Son as an atoning sacrifice for our
sins...We love because he first loved us.
1 JOHN 4:10,19

Some of my favorite movies and songs have themes about love, like *The Notebook, P.S. I Love You,* or Taylor Swift's song "Love Story."

We love *love* so much because it's at the core of who we are. We need love just like the air we breathe! A girl in today's world can easily look for love in a boyfriend, thinking that the perfect guy will make her truly happy. But no man in this life will ever meet the deepest longings of a woman's heart. Jesus is the only one who can do that.

Real love is found only in God. Even sex is not love; it's only an expression of love between a man and wife. The Bible says that God displayed true love when He "sent his Son as an atoning sacrifice for our sins." It also says God is love (1 John 4:8).

Jesus gave another example of love in John 15:13: "Greater love has no one than this, that he lay down his life for his friends." Our focus verse and John 15:13 sound alike. Both contain selfless qualities. Can you imagine putting this into practice? Maybe you can. Maybe you have saved a toddler from drowning or an elderly person from getting hit by a car. Maybe you know a soldier who willingly fights for our country, laying down his life for his friends. This is what Jesus did for us. He laid down His life willingly for us, His friends.

The apostle Paul describes this kind of love:

> Love is patient, love is kind. It does not envy, it does not boast, it is not proud. It is not rude, it is not self-seeking, it is not easily angered, it keeps no record of wrongs. Love does not delight in evil but rejoices with the truth. It always protects, always trusts, always hopes, always perseveres. Love never fails (1 Corinthians 13:4-8).

There is nothing selfish in that passage. That's because love is selfless. True love puts the other's needs first. It's amazing! Can you imagine the impact we would have if we demonstrated the true love of Christ every day? Our lives would radically change. Even our world would change! Let's commit today to show His love to those around us and make a difference!

What's a Girl to Do?

Living out of the true love of God requires us to put our wants aside. We would change our lives and the world if we lived out of true love. Love is powerful! Let's challenge ourselves this week to truly love.

Totally Talkin' with God

Father, You are love. Without You, we have no love. Thank You that through my faith in Jesus, You live in me. I want to live out Your love and impact my world for You! In Jesus' name, amen.

America's Idols

You shall have no other gods before Me.
DEUTERONOMY 5:7 NASB

J ust from this title, I bet you know what I'm going to talk about in this devotional! Kelly Clarkson, Reuben Studdard, Carrie Underwood, Taylor Hicks, Jordin Sparks, David Cook, Kris Allen... One of the most popular television shows right now is *American Idol*. (Yes, I admit I watch it!)

In reality, idolizing happens everywhere. Zeus. Buddha. Muhammad. Mother Earth. People have created and worshipped thousands of gods over the years all around the world.

What about you? What or whom do you worship? The Sunday school answer is Jesus. But is that true for you?

I found this in a *Relevant* magazine article: "A thirteen-year-old California girl has racked up 14,528 text messages in one month. Most of the messages are sent to one of four friends. Apparently, the average number of monthly texts for a 13- to 17-year-old teen is 1,742...that's a lot of LOL."

My dad has always said (and now I find myself saying as well), "You can tell a person's priorities in life by where she spends her time and who she spends it with." There are so many things out there competing for our time, like Facebook, our cell phones, MySpace, video games, the Internet, hours of homework...you know what I mean! It's difficult to find time to spend with God. And He is often last on the list.

Think about it. What gets between you and God? Let's face it—it's not easy being totally God's. We lose focus on Him and turn to other things to find significance and self-worth. Boys make us feel loved. Brand-name clothes and cute shoes make us feel beautiful. And listening to the popular music, watching great movies, and reading gossip magazines make us feel connected. We want to belong and be loved.

In our search for belonging, we can often give too much of ourselves. In our longing for someone to see us, we can become obsessed with hairstyle, makeup, clothes, and so on. We may even lose ourselves in the hope to be noticed.

What are you spending your time doing? Talking on the phone? Shopping? Texting? Facebooking? Dating? Playing sports? Participating in clubs or organizations? Making perfect grades on homework?

I admit these are not horrible things to do. But how are you doing with prayer, Bible reading, living in community with solid Christian friends and church members, listening to encouraging sermons, and other things we know will bring us closer to God?

All of us desire to be intimately known, understood, accepted, loved. But God already intimately knows us, loves us, understands us, and accepts us just the way we are. (See Psalm 139:13-16.)

If you have put God on the back burner and have focused more time and energy on the things of this world than on your growth in Him, take time today to honestly admit this to yourself and to God. Ask Him to show you areas of your life that need reprioritizing. You may feel bad when you finally realize how you've been spending your time, but this conviction is good. It's from the Holy Spirit, and it will help lead you to change. Strive to spend time with God on a daily basis if you are not already doing so. You will be blessed, and your relationship with God will begin to grow stronger each day. Now is the best time to begin!

What's a Girl to Do?

Letting go of our idols is difficult. But through Jesus, we can do all things. Begin to focus your eyes and heart on Christ and let the idols fall!

Totally Talkin' with God

Father, please help me. I want to quit worrying and caring about what this world tells me to, but change is difficult. I need You to help steer my mind toward the things of You. I desire to believe that You intimately know me and love me enough to die for me. Open my eyes and heart so that I may understand the truth. In Jesus' name, amen.

Dating a Non-Christian

Do not be yoked together with unbelievers. For what
do righteousness and wickedness have in common? Or
what fellowship can light have with darkness?

2 CORINTHIANS 6:14

Have you ever thought, *Why am I so focused on boys?* Have you ever wondered what is really behind our anxiety, why we think we need to act now or lose out on the men of our dreams? I have!

Some girls are taught that all they need is God and they shouldn't think about boys at all. As a result, they feel ashamed and guilty just for having feelings for boys.

Let me explain. God created Eve because He knew that it was not good for man to be alone. We were created for relationships. Having a boyfriend is not necessarily a problem. You are not unspiritual if you are interested in boys. The problem comes when our interest in boys consumes us.

When our desire to have a boyfriend is all we can think about, we become easy targets for the enemy. We become tempted to settle on whatever boy shows interest in us. Boundaries we established and standards we set become blurred. We can even drop the standard to date only Christians.

Are you familiar with the term *missionary dating*? It's used when someone who is a believer wants to date a nonbeliever in order to witness to him. Yeah, right! That's probably not going to happen!

How important is it that we date only Christian guys? It's very important! Our focus verse says not to be yoked or united with an unbeliever. We might paraphrase Paul as saying, "Hey, what do you have in common with those who do things against God? It's like mixing the temple of God with idols. That just shouldn't happen. Walk with God. Be separate from them. Be pure and stay away from the things that will lead you to bad decisions" (2 Corinthians 6:17–7:1).

The main reason not to date unbelievers is that God doesn't want us to compromise our relationship with Him—for anything or anyone! You can't be neutral with God. You're either hot or cold. On or off. For God or against Him. God wants you to make a choice and stick with it.

Dating a guy who is not placing Jesus first in his life is going to make it hard for you to keep Him first in yours. He may even say things like, "Hey babe, I won't tell anyone. Just this once, okay. Please? I love you." At that point, you could melt. Or you may be able to say no the first few times, but not every time. It's like playing with fire. If you play with it long enough, you are going to get burned.

The man you marry one day will be your teammate for life. It's very hard to work as a team when you have different goals and beliefs.

Make a commitment today to remain firm and set a standard to date only Christian guys. Begin to focus on strengthening your relationship with God so that the only guys you will attract will be those with the same determination—to honor and glorify God above all. It's the secret to building a winning team that will go the distance for life!

What's a Girl to Do?

You may have household rules on dating. Maybe you are not allowed to date until you're 16 or 18. That can be hard, but your parents have set that boundary for a reason. If you want to understand, calmly ask them about it. Whatever you do, don't jump into relationships just to be loved. And if your parents let you date, I encourage you to make it a top priority that he be a Christian.

Totally Talkin' with God

Father, help me to be so focused on my relationship with You that boys will have to chase You to find me. In Jesus' name, amen.

9

EMOTIONS
AND ATTITUDE

Devotions on how to focus our passion and mind on Christ

Drama Queen

It was for freedom that Christ set us free; therefore keep
standing firm and do not be subject again to a yoke of slavery.
GALATIANS 5:1 NASB

Have you ever seen the movie *Confessions of a Teenage Drama Queen*? Very funny! "So much drama, so little time." I know you know what I'm talking about. To this kind of girl, everything's a major production. She loves attention, and the world is her stage. Given the chance to perform, she will shine every time!

A drama queen is a female who talks a lot, cries a lot, and laughs a lot, all in the same five minutes. When she gets to school and notices her fingernail polish is chipped, the whole day is ruined. When the family car is being fixed and she can't go shopping after school, the world is going to end. You get the picture.

I've known some drama queens. They provide great entertainment, but I wonder what is really going on underneath the drama act. *What is she trying to hide? Why doesn't she want us to see the real her?*

Acting takes a lot of work. Constantly having to be something you're not can drain the energy right out of you. You can exhaust yourself by always making sure you're ready to perform at any minute, always watching for everyone's reactions.

Have you ever made a decision based on what you felt in the moment? I have. It's easy to fall into the trap of immediately acting on our feelings, especially when we are hurt. Sure, if we've been genuinely hurt, we'll be angry, jealous, or sad. That's normal. We all feel that way. But our feelings don't have to lead to drama.

We must be careful not to base our decisions on what we're feeling at the moment. Our feelings are important, and we need to pay attention to them. But we also need to stop and think about why we feel the way we do before we act. Otherwise, we set ourselves up for further disappointment and hurt. Immediately acting on our feelings can lead to actions we will later regret deeply—and our sudden choices may even damage those we love most.

God knows we will get riled up. He created us with passions that run deep within our souls, stirring up our emotions. Our job, as followers of Christ, is to ask for His help to control these emotions so we don't make bad decisions in light of our feelings.

God has freed you from the power of sin and the power of your emotions. Praise Jesus! You don't have to be a drama queen—you can be free to be the real you!

What's a Girl to Do?

If you struggle with being an emotional decision maker, remember the freedom we have in Christ. We don't have to be ruled by our emotions. Let's challenge ourselves to make decisions based on our reality in Christ.

Totally Talkin' with God

Father, thank You for Your unending forgiveness! You have made me a passionate young woman, but I don't want to be a drama queen. I trust You to help me identify areas where I struggle. I trust that I can do all things through Christ. Regardless of the results, I know You love me! In Jesus' name, amen.

&$%*#@

Do not neglect doing good and sharing, for
with such sacrifices God is pleased.
HEBREWS 13:16 NASB

I was recently riding through Colorado with my family. I must have been the only one who saw a small sign that said Dam Road. As Dad turned onto the road and began to cross a gigantic reservoir, I couldn't resist: "Dam Road is long, isn't it." He turned around and nearly wrecked us. When I showed him the name of the road, we all laughed!

Have you ever heard of No Cussing Clubs? Apparently, a 14-year-old guy named McKay Hatch formed the club when he got tired of all the profanity around him. His family did not allow such language, and McKay got sick of hearing it all the time. He vowed to throw four-letter words out of his own vocabulary, and he encouraged others to do the same.

McKay goes to South Pasadena High School, and his club meets on Wednesdays. They have a website, matching orange shirts, and a hip-hop theme song. Many others have followed his lead. In fact, researchers estimate that nearly 20,000 people have joined similar clubs.

You think McKay doesn't take heat for it? He gets persecuted all of the time for not cussing. Can you believe that? People stop by his club meetings, fire off a few mouth bombs, and leave. He and his family have also been the targets of hate mail and even death threats.

The Bible tells us the tongue is like a flame that can burn an entire forest down if not controlled. It also gives the image of our tongue as the rudder of a giant ship. With the smallest movement of a tiny rudder (or our tongues), an entire boat (or our bodies and minds) can be moved off course (James 3:4-6).

God doesn't want us to give up on speaking, but if you have a bad habit, He can help you overcome it. We all stumble in many ways. But to throw around dirty words is not only trashy and tacky but also ungodly.

Instead, think of all the good we can do with our words and deeds. I'm not talking about being a goody-goody, but about being godly. Practice today saying encouraging words that build people up instead of tear them down. (See Ephesians 4:29.) We are called to a higher standard than the world is. We must be willing to be different, to be like Christ. If you want to be totally God's, you need to speak that way.

What's a Girl to Do?

We are not McKay Hatch, but we are daughters of God. With the Holy Spirit living in us, let's challenge ourselves to love others. Let's please God even more with our behavior!

Totally Talkin' with God

Father, I am totally into being Yours. Show me what that means. Guide me into a closer relationship with You. Reveal areas of my life that I need to ditch and replace with the goodness of Christ. I want this, but I can't do it without Your help. Hold my hand, Lord. In Jesus' name, amen.

Who? What? Me?

Don't fret or worry. Instead of worrying, pray. Let petitions and
praises shape your worries into prayers, letting God know your
concerns. Before you know it, a sense of God's wholeness, everything
coming together for good, will come and settle you down. It's wonderful
what happens when Christ displaces worry at the center of your life.
PHILIPPIANS 4:6-7 MSG

If you've ever been on a blind date, you may relate to this story—but I really hope not!

My friends had set me up with a really cute guy. They asked me to join them for a movie and said he would be there. Oh my! I was completely freaked out!

One problem—they didn't tell him I was coming. And that's not all. My friends, trying to hook me up, told the guy I liked him.

When I showed up at the movie theater, the guy ignored me all night long. Talk about awkward! I began to worry that he didn't like me or that I had a major defect that made me unlovable or undesirable. I had dressed cute and thought I looked nice, but when he ran, I just knew it was my fault. *Do I have a huge zit on my face?* I wondered. *Did my hair frizz? Did I have bad breath or say something stupid?* I became consumed with what went wrong.

I told my mom what had happened. She looked straight at me and asked, "What's wrong with him?"

I told her it was me, not the guy.

She disagreed. "He ran away. That's childish."

Looking back at that night, I now notice how easy it is to become worried when we lose control of a situation, to be anxious when things don't go the way we planned. Is this common? Yes. Is it healthy? Not really.

When we know something is coming, we worry.

When we don't know what is coming, we worry.

And worry causes stress, making us grumpy and unbearable for those we love.

So how do we learn to de-stress our lives? Read today's verse. Pray about *everything*. Give thanks, even when things are bad. Does this mean you won't be anxious at times? Not at all. But it does mean you have a place to take your anxiety. Now read the last sentence in verse 5. The NIV says, "God is near." When we rely on God through prayer, we can trust He is near us whether our circumstances are as minimal as a bad date or as serious as a sick parent, divorce, or even abuse. God is near.

There is no better time than the present to begin a good habit, and one of the best habits we can cultivate is to push aside anxious thoughts and replace them with prayers of thanksgiving. Listen to the advice of an anonymous quote I came across: "Never trouble trouble till trouble troubles you." We'll give trouble a run for its money when we don't react with worry, but with solid trust in our mighty God!

What's a Girl to Do?

Put Philippians 4:6-7 into action this week. When we begin to worry, let's do what these verses recommend. Pray. Give thanks. And do so repeatedly. Then trust that God will do the rest!

Totally Talkin' with God

Father, this world comes with so much trouble. Anxiety is easy to feel, even on a daily basis. I don't want to be an anxious person. Instead, I want to trust in You, God. Help me to begin to do so by following what Your Word says in Philippians 4. I love you, Lord! In Jesus' name, amen.

Are You Satisfied?

I know how to get along with humble means, and I also know how to
live in prosperity; in any and every circumstance I have learned the
secret of being filled and going hungry, both of having abundance and
suffering need. I can do all things through Him who strengthens me.
PHILIPPIANS 4:12-13 NASB

What makes you content? The newest pair of Rocket Dog shoes? Brand-new jeans? What about a contact list full of friends who love to text and just hang out? A boyfriend who really cares and, by the way, looks good?

Let me tell you the story of Ella.

Ella worked as a missionary with pygmies in Africa for 52 years. Mimi, Ella's daughter, wondered how her mother endured the scorching heat and sweltering humidity with such a positive attitude. Then Mimi came across her mother's journal and read this list:

- Never allow yourself to complain about anything—not even the weather.
- Never picture yourself in any other circumstance or some-place else.
- Never compare your lot with another's.
- Never allow yourself to wish this or that had been otherwise.
- Never dwell on tomorrow—remember that [tomorrow] is God's, not ours.

The apostle Paul lived a torturous life after his conversion to Jesus. He suffered shipwrecks, torture, imprisonment, beatings, and more. How did he remain so content? I doubt he had Ella's list of recommended habits, but I do think he and Ella drew their contentment from the same place. Here's the NIV rendering of today's verses: "I know what it is to be in need, and I know what it is to have plenty. I have learned the secret of being content in any and every situation, whether well fed or hungry, whether living in plenty or in want. I can do everything through him who gives me strength" (Philippians 4:12-13).

As a young woman, you may have plenty. Or you may be in want. Generally, our generation is pampered and taken care of more than any before it. I am quite confident that nearly every young woman reading this devotional today has some sort of electronic gadget—an iPod, cell phone, TV, DVD player, or computer.

Without a question, we have been given much. But with all that we have, I wonder—are we really content? And what about less concrete things? What else do you do to feel satisfied in life? Do you hide behind your good grades? Your sports achievements? Your beautiful voice? Your looks? Do you compare yourself to others, discontent because you don't have what they do?

Contentment in such areas comes easy when life is going well. But how do you do when things get difficult? Where do you go to calm or soothe yourself in stressful times? To feel satisfied and safe again?

Paul and Ella had contentment. They were satisfied in the good times and bad. Not that we should never be discontent—in fact, discontentment can lead to positive change. But when our discontent leads to coveting, stress, and turning to things other than the Lord, it's like telling God we don't trust Him. He wants us to be content in all things, knowing that He is trustworthy. In the good, the bad, and the ugly. Doing so makes us a little more like Paul and Ella. A little more like Christ.

What's a Girl to Do?

Let's try to be content in our own circumstances. Maybe we could drop the minutes on our cell or texts and use the money to sponsor a child or do something else great in Jesus' name. Doing so may help us be content wherever Christ has us.

Totally Talkin' with God

Father, You freely give me good gifts. You provide me with comforts and even most of my wants. Your love is great, and I thank You. Help me to be content regardless of my circumstances and to reach out to those who are in need. In Jesus' name, amen.

Knowing Who (and Whose) You Are

Whatever you do, do your work heartily, as
for the Lord rather than for men.

The phone rings. You jump out of the shower and wrap a towel around yourself. *I hope this isn't Shelly canceling our plans for tonight. I'm so looking forward to hanging out.*

Running late, you pick up the phone in a flurry. "Hello?" you say while towel drying your hair.

"Hi. I really need your help tonight..." The voice on the other end is from a good friend—a friend who often asks for your help. And because you are so nice and everyone likes that about you, you never say no.

"Oh?" you answer hesitantly. *What?* Your brain screams. *I already have plans. This can't be happening.* "What did you need?"

"I really need someone to babysit my brother and sister for me," your friend says. "I have to help Holly. She's really sad and needs to talk."

So tell her she can talk to you while you both *watch your brother and sister,* you think to yourself.

Have you ever been in this situation? What would you do? You so want to be liked, you in no way want to create any waves with anybody, and now here you are with a dilemma. You're in the middle of two friends. Tough call, right?

Look at Jesus' example for a moment. During His ministry, He visited His hometown. Did they throw Him a party? Have a big celebration? Greet Him like a king? No, they did the opposite. These were the people who saw Jesus as a child. They were friends with His normal, sinful family. They wondered how He could be the promised Messiah. After all, He was the son of Joseph—the local carpenter.

Knowing who He was, that He *was* the promised one, allowed Jesus to make decisions accordingly—regardless of what others thought, regardless of what they believed. Jesus boldly proclaimed who He was and what He stood for. Those in his own hometown got mad, even threatening to throw him off a cliff. So what did Jesus do? He made his way through the angry crowd and left. Jesus was going to preach elsewhere.

Jesus was *not* a people pleaser. He was a God pleaser. He knew not only who He was but also whose He was.

I don't know about you, but this is hard for me. I want to make others happy. I often spend so much time trying to please people that sometimes I lose sight of myself. It can leave me feeling angry at somebody—usually myself.

We should do good to all, as we have a chance (Galatians 6:10). But something is wrong if you become miserable and begin to lose your own identity. Once you discover who you are—and whose you are—you no longer have to seek other people's approval, just God's (Galatians 1:10).

What's a Girl to Do?

Let's make an effort this week to please God first. You may want to do something for Him that others won't see (so they won't be able to praise you). Then you can bask in the knowledge that God is happy with your good choice!

Totally Talkin' with God

Father, thank You for loving me! I enjoy learning about You and what You are like. Give me wisdom so I can deal kindly with others. Help me to always do Your good, pleasing, and perfect will. In Jesus' name, amen.

Tomorrow

Now listen, you who say, "Today or tomorrow we will go to this or
that city, spend a year there, carry on business and make money."
Why, you do not even know what will happen tomorrow...Instead,
you ought to say, "If it is the Lord's will, we will live and do this
or that." As it is, you boast and brag. All such boasting is evil.
JAMES 4:13-16

My mom loves lists. If we're throwing a party, she has lists of people, food, expenses, you name it. If we go grocery shopping, she has a list. If we go on vacation, she has a list. If she tells dad to do something, she gives him a list (which he always either loses or ignores). My mom loves to be organized and in control.

Do you? Most of us do. We have short-term and long-term goals. And this is great. But what happens when something unexpected comes along, like a sickness? Or maybe a friend or family member calls in need. Or maybe you don't make the team.

I've struggled with this time and again. Many times, I want things my way. But when things don't go my way and I remain inflexible, I get irritable and unpleasant to be around. Listen to today's verse in The Message:

Now I have a word for you who brashly announce, "Today—at
the latest, tomorrow—we're off to such and such city for the
year. We're going to start a business and make a lot of money."
You don't know the first thing about tomorrow. You're nothing
but a wisp of fog, catching a brief bit of sun before disappearing.
Instead, make it a habit to say, "If the Master wills it, and we're
still alive, we'll do this or that."

If I had to guess, I would say James was a pretty straightforward guy. He cut to the chase and laid it all out on the table for everyone to see. Maybe he had heard Christians talk as if they ran their lives themselves and he wanted to help them understand that God is the one who really guides our steps. (See Proverbs 16:9.)

Jesus preached a similar message. "Do not worry about tomorrow, for tomorrow will worry about itself. Each day has enough trouble of its own" (Matthew 6:33-34).

I'm not advocating giving up your planner. I'm suggesting that we hold our plans loosely, acknowledge God's overall control, surrender to do His will above all, and sit back and see what happens. It may not be what we expected or desired. My guess is it will be better in the end than anything *we* could have penciled down!

What's a Girl to Do?

Most of us have some kind of planner, BlackBerry, or iPhone that helps us plan our days, weeks, and months. As I said, we don't have to trash them. We just need to have the attitude that God is really in control. We are to trust in Him. Let's do it!

Totally Talkin' with God

Father, I love You! No one is more capable to order my life than You are. You may plan things I do not expect, but I trust in Your goodness. Help me to keep an attitude like Christ's. I give it to You, Lord. Be my personal organizer. In Jesus' name, amen.

Humility or Humiliation? You Choose

Do you want to stand out? Then step down. Be a servant. If you
puff yourself up, you'll get the wind knocked out of you. But if you're
content to simply be yourself, your life will count for plenty.
MATTHEW 23:12 MSG

Remember *Spider-Man 3*? The gorgeous redheaded Kirsten Dunst is Spider-Man's girl. The totally cute Tobey Maguire is Spider-Man. However, in this particular movie, Spider-Man is not so cute. The underlying theme is a battle between his good nature (servanthood and love) and evil nature (pride and a hunger for power).

Spider-Man's pride causes him to lose touch with those who matter most to him. As a result, his most important relationships break, leaving him desperate and alone. In his love of power, he neglects his most cherished relationships.

Do you want to stand out for Christ? Do you want to be used in great ways for His glory? Then you must learn the meaning of humility.

I'm not saying we all need to be doormats. Being humble doesn't mean being quiet or weak. It simply means we realize that without God, we would be nothing. A humble person is always aware of who He is (God) and who we are (God's servants). Living this way, we will be content, and our life can really count for God.

Pride is just about the opposite. A prideful girl doesn't think she needs to compare herself to anyone because no one would measure up to her. If she does make comparisons, she looks down on others as inferior to her. Pride is ultimately a result of selfishness. When we only focus on ourselves and forget that we are created by the Creator, we become prideful about what we think we have achieved. We think it is all of our own doing and not blessing from God.

Setting the perfect example, Jesus humbly bore the sins of the world in total humility. He was the King of kings, yet He humbled Himself enough to come to our world as a human. Even more, He was willing to

174 Totally **God's** 4 Life Devotional

die the most humiliating death imaginable. Now *that's* true love, sacrifice, and humility!

The Bible warns us to humble ourselves. I think we have no other choice. Either we humble ourselves or God and others will humble us. Pride will humiliate you, but humility will honor you. To be totally God's is to practice humility.

What's a Girl to Do?

Sometimes the most humble act is to allow an honor to pass over us. I have no idea what activities you are pursuing or whether you are prideful or humble. Let's pray that God would show us how to act out true humility this week in service to others for His glory!

Totally Talkin' with God

Father, thank You for Your example of humility in Jesus. The world is so full of pride that I easily forget I am not of the world and don't have to be like it. Through the power of the Holy Spirit, please give me a humble heart. In Jesus' name, amen.

Whom Do You Love?

"YOU SHALL LOVE THE LORD YOUR GOD WITH ALL YOUR
HEART, AND WITH ALL YOUR SOUL, AND WITH ALL
YOUR MIND." This is the great and foremost commandment.
MATTHEW 22:37-38 NASB

We are a generation and a nation that likes to indulge ourselves. Whatever catches our attention on television, in magazines, or through other media sources soon becomes our obsession. We have to have that new haircut to match Taylor Swift's, the shoes like Miley Cyrus's, or the new music by Hilary Duff. Look at all the money Americans spend on advertising—billions! And it's all put into enticing us to desire or *love* a product.

It's easy to say we *love* our new hoodie or cute toe ring we bought at Target. But what are we really saying? Not that we *love* the item we bought, but that we love how it makes us feel and look. We want to be noticed, and we easily become infatuated with *loving* things because they make us feel and look lovely.

That may be twisted and hard to understand, but what I'm trying to get across is this: We absolutely *must* keep love real. As girls who are totally God's, we know whom Jesus calls us to love. Jesus explains that we should love the Lord our God first. Then we should love our neighbor.

God gives us the capacity to love not only Him but also those around us. The tricky part is learning how to love Him first. In my opinion, we begin to love God first when we spend time with Him. We pray, read the Bible, and worship and praise His name. As we do, our love for God grows. And soon, He is first in our lives.

I think one of the greatest parts about loving God first is that our eyes are opened. We can't help but see and know His love for all of mankind. We realize more than ever how much Jesus loved us.

Whom and what do you love? Where and with whom do you spend most of your time? Love is powerful, and it is meant for good. Love God and love people—that's being totally God's!

What's a Girl to Do?

Together, let's commit to seek God first by talking with Him daily, trusting in His faithfulness, reading His Word, worshipping Him, and obeying His commands. Love God and love others!

Totally Talkin' with God

Father, I so want You to be my first love. I want to love You with all my heart, soul, and mind, Lord. That is the ultimate—to be in an intimate relationship with You, my God who created me with love and for love! In Jesus' name, amen.

Where Do We Go from Here?

Thanks for joining me on this journey of being totally God's!

Continuing along this path will take commitment. Be sure to find other Christian books and devotionals to supplement your Bible reading. Know of my love and prayers for you. Never quit and never compromise. God really loves you and has a dream for your life. Press in close to Him, and I know you will be free to live it out every day!

Warmly,